BRAND BREAKTHROUGH

How to go beyond a catchy tagline to build
an authentic, influential and sustainable
brand personality

Margie Agin

ISBN: 978-0-578-44062-0

For Doris Poltilove, who loved language

Table of Contents

INTRODUCTION TO BRAND PERSONALITY

Your customers don't care about you. They're busy, distracted people fighting to keep up in an increasingly noisy world. Many companies try to break through the noise by getting—well—louder! With so many voices yelling at them, it's no wonder people run for the hills.

Creating more content isn't the answer. These days, content must be fiercely compelling for people to read, share and link to it. When your audience has seen a similar ad, webpage or presentation 100 times before, they glaze over and your message gets lost. Over two-thirds of content never gets seen![1]

The world is cluttered with boring companies telling generic stories. Don't contribute to the junk pile.

Be different. Stand out. Take a stand.

The power of brand personality has helped organizations differentiate themselves, influence buyers and achieve rapid growth. Using the lessons outlined in this book, you can do the same.

Why brand personality?

Almost half of Americans and 84% of millennials mistrust brands.[2] So, how can your brand earn their trust and communicate with them more effectively?

People buy from people. To build powerful connections with your audience, you must make your brand seem more like a person—a person defined by character traits that guide how you present yourself to the world.

Even business-to-business (B2B) companies are actually *people* selling to *people*. They aren't excused from having a brand personality. Throughout this book you'll see numerous examples that demonstrate how B2B companies use brand personality to their advantage.

Elements of brand personality

An authentic brand personality builds a genuine connection between a company and its customers based on open, honest communication. Your brand personality is intrinsic to your organization. It reflects your company culture and the experience you create for everyone interacting with you.

Brand personality isn't simply about visual brand identity (logo, colors, photography, etc.). Those things are important elements that support your brand, but they come after your core brand personality is defined. If you've ever been handed a beautifully designed webpage with *Lorem Ipsum* copy as a placeholder, you know what I'm talking about. You can't just fill the blank spaces on that page with any old copy.

The strongest, most persuasive brand personalities employ carefully selected messages and language to build authority and connect with customers emotionally and intellectually.

In this book we'll break down the process of developing a brand personality into a step-by-step playbook. We'll focus on how your brand personality impacts *what you say* and *how you say it.*

- *What you say* includes marketing messages, promises and examples.

- *How you say it* refers to language choices, tone and format.

Who is this book for? Who should care about brand personality?

Marketing teams are typically considered the caretakers of the company's brand because they're responsible for producing and distributing the vast majority of content. In most cases, the marketing team does the work to articulate and document the brand personality.

But branding isn't something that should be discussed in the vacuum of a marketing meeting and then get handed down from the mountaintop to the rest of the organization. The most consistent brands reflect all areas of a company and are built with input from different groups.

Company leaders

When a company is in high growth mode, its culture is most at risk. It's a vital time for leaders to understand and articulate the company culture they want to maintain. In the same vein, this is the time when customer loyalty presents the most risk and the most potential. If you can consistently convey an authentic brand personality even as your company grows, you can retain customers and turn them into passionate brand advocates, with measurable impact on revenue.

Sales teams

Sales teams have an incredibly important role in defining and maintaining a company's brand. They're the voice and face of the organization and must embody the brand in the words they choose and the actions they take. During the brand development process, part of their role is to be a conduit for communication between customers and the rest of the organization. A salesperson can tell if brand messages are getting customers excited or if the messages are falling flat.

Product and technical teams

Most technical folks, developers and engineers spend their time ensuring things work, not thinking about how people *feel* about their experience. But if you have a tangible product you're selling—hardware, software or consumer good—the experience customers have with that product is a component of your brand's personality. Let's say a company wants its brand to embody "simplicity." A user interface that's complex and messy reflects poorly on the brand.

Human Resources teams

In a tight job market, HR teams need to consider the "talent brand" of their organization as part of their recruiting and retention strategies. People are increasingly looking for work that makes an impact. According to the 2018 *Global Brand Health Report*, companies that communicate their brand personality get more attention from potential employees.[3] LinkedIn reported in *The Employer Brand Playbook* that a strong talent brand reduces cost-per-hire by up to 50% and can slash turnover rates by as much as 28%.[4]

Anyone who writes or hires writers

On a practical level, creating and documenting your brand personality saves time creating sales and marketing materials. Once you have defined your brand personality and created guidelines and parameters, you can hand off to content creators and they can start creating without having to reinvent the wheel. That includes copywriters, technical product writers, social media managers, email marketers and SEO specialists.

Visual and UX designers

Logos, colors, typeface, photography and page layout choices need to be in synch with your brand personality. For example, you don't want to marry a cartoon-like graphic style with a serious tone of voice in your writing. Designers must intimately understand the traits of the brand personality to do their work.

What's different about *this* approach to branding?

This book was born from a personal frustration with the gap between "top-down" brand strategy and consistent, sustainable execution.

Most brand projects operate in what I think of as the brand stratosphere. They take a 10,000-foot view of brand from the top down. Their main goal is to build awareness, or what is sometimes called "air cover," for the rest of the organization to do the so-called "real work."

I don't come from that world. I came to brand marketing from the ground up. I started out in market research, which is about as ground up in the marketing world as you can get. I was on the phone, interviewing business leaders, engineers, purchasing agents and other decision makers about how they select and use products. I learned to talk to basically anyone about basically anything, from HR software to milking machines, and find patterns and hot buttons to transform into marketing messages.

Years later, having conducted hundreds of interviews with customers and subject matter experts and all different types of research projects, I'm convinced that direct conversations are essential to the decision-making process.

I've built and led teams through times of rapid change. I've managed brand launches as an internal marketing leader and as an external marketing strategist with Centerboard Marketing. After executing a brand refresh, companies I work with have experienced tremendous growth. The brand personality process in this book has helped them clarify their unique position in the market and improve how customers interact with their website and content throughout the sales process.

Some businesses measure success in terms of lead generation; commonly web conversion rates more than double after a brand refresh. Armed with qualified leads and sales enablement content that accelerates the buying cycle, companies I work with have experienced record sales. A global video conferencing provider quadrupled in size and reached over $1 billion in revenue. A cyber security company achieved 240% growth in a core product line year over year. My start-up clients have attracted attention from the market thanks to their crisp, differentiated messaging and have experienced successful acquisitions with higher-than-expected valuations.

That's why this book starts with steps that create a stable foundation for an authentic brand personality. Essentially, we'll work from the ground up.

To that end, this book is divided into eight chapters:

- Chapters 1-3 outline strategic decisions that guide your planning and set you on the right course.

- Chapters 4-6 detail proven techniques to develop and hone your brand personality.

- Chapters 7-8 cover key considerations and inspiration for your rollout and ongoing brand execution.

I recommend progressing through the steps as they're presented in the book. The basic process would be the same regardless of your company's size. If you're small and nimble, you may move faster because you have fewer decision makers to align. On the other hand, if you've never before considered the questions that we'll explore in this book, it could take longer to work through the process.

Hands-on activities and your free action guide

This book isn't designed to create a brand statemont that never leaves a marketing meeting or a binder of ideas that simply sit on a shelf.

Instead, it's a framework to help companies develop a structure for a brand personality that will be sustainable over time. It includes some "gotchas" that can derail your brand work—lessons learned the hard way that you can avoid.

Before we get too far, make sure you get your free *Brand Breakthrough Action Guide* at www. centerboard-marketing.com/brand-breakthrough-action-guide. As you progress through the stages outlined in the book, you'll be able to refer to the guide for ready-made templates and activities you can customize and complete for your organization.

By the end of this book, you'll have all the tools necessary to define and implement a unique brand personality. You'll be ready to help your company take the next step forward in its growth, stand out from the crowd and build powerful customer relationships. Even if you've never worked on a brand project before, the examples and techniques within will give you the confidence to lead the process.

This is the first step of a journey

In our day-to-day work lives, it's tempting to sweep brand questions under the rug in favor of an impending deadline or solving the next crisis. A brand project forces you to examine core questions that are difficult to answer. This journey takes time and willingness to stop the treadmill.

Along the way, there will be twists and turns. You may hit some dead ends and have to double back. Don't let fear, lethargy, or lack of confidence get in the way of taking the first step on the journey.

If you don't define your brand, others will define it for you

Companies without a strong brand personality end up being passive participants in their own marketing. Prospective customers make assumptions about them. Salespeople start telling inconsistent, confusing stories. Worse, competitors paint an unflattering picture they struggle to defend against.

Don't procrastinate. It's time to define and launch your brand personality. I hope you're fired up and ready to go!

CHAPTER 1
SETTING YOUR GOALS

What you'll learn in this chapter: We'll kick things off with three real-life examples of organizations struggling to achieve their goals. By comparing and contrasting their communication choices, you'll feel the impact a strong brand personality can make.

Your brand personality is one of the most important levers you can use to make a qualitative and quantitative impact on your business.

Every year, Interbrand publishes a report ranking the top global brands as determined by internal factors (clarity, commitment, protection and responsiveness) and external factors (authenticity, relevance, differentiation, consistency, presence and understanding). When we overlay the performance of Interbrand's 40 top-ranked brands against the MSCI World Index, we see they outperform the market, with 73% greater return to shareholders.[5]

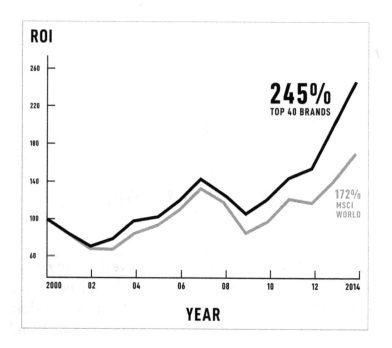

In addition to shareholder value, there are many other business objectives a powerful brand personality can help achieve. The more you clarify your goals up front, the easier it will be to make decisions, prioritize actions and measure success.

Many organizations turn to brand projects out of fear or embarrassment. They're afraid to send people to their website because it's inaccurate or out of date. Others face external pressure, such as shifting market dynamics or increased competition, and look to brand projects to address their challenges. Before you embark on a brand personality project, ask yourself: What do we hope to gain after our brand personality is launched? Why is *this* the right time?

Brand development is part art and part science. As much as possible, make your goals measurable so you can report on your progress. Determine what metrics you can collect and track over time. Even qualitative goals such as "brand perception" can become measurable with the right scoring system.

Measurable goals impacted by your brand personality can include:

- Sales volume, revenue and customer mix

- Customer referral and retention rates

- Number of customers switching from competitors

- Website engagement and conversion rates

- Hiring ability

- Social media sentiment

- Operational efficiencies, such as cost savings and production time

- Employee satisfaction rates

To demonstrate success, you can report on metrics before and after your brand personality rollout. You can also show how your organization compares to direct competitors or others in your cohort (as in the Interbrand analysis).

Let's ground this discussion in some real-life examples that demonstrate how a well-crafted and well-executed brand personality helps organizations achieve their business goals.

Verizon vs. Sprint

Let's take the examples of two communications industry behemoths—Verizon and Sprint. We can assume both have large marketing teams and budgets most of us would give our right kidney to have. This should make brand development a snap, right? Not exactly.

Sometimes size makes it easier to build a brand, but often it makes agreement and execution more challenging. Large companies have siloed organizations and many competing interests. They can get stuck in old ways of doing things and avoid taking risks.

In this case, both Verizon and Sprint have business units that sell wireless services to small business. They're targeting the same type of buyer—the small business owner who needs connectivity to run operations and communicate with customers. Essentially, they offer the same types of services and pricing is ultracompetitive. What's more, Verizon is consistently rated higher than Sprint in terms of network speed, coverage and reliability.[6]

How can Sprint compete?

Sprint leverages brand personality to build an emotional connection with customers that differentiates it from Verizon.

Here is a snippet from a Verizon webpage promoting its wireless services to small businesses.

In a small company, every minute counts, and leveraging mobile technology is an important component of modern business. Whether they're located in Denver or Dubai, small businesses today need fast, reliable Internet connections that allow people to work virtually anywhere, on any device. An effective Wi-Fi service keeps everyone—from employees to visiting clients and customers—connected and productive. This sea change in the way we live and work is here to stay.

In the office, workers need the flexibility to be able to take their laptop to the conference room, down the hall, or to a sister site to collaborate without losing connectivity. To stay productive, they need to stay connected whether they're on the road, working remotely, or traveling. Likewise, clients expect that when they reach out to your business, someone will be available to answer questions promptly and be responsive to their needs immediately. Visiting customers and clients also want to stay Internet-enabled when they're visiting your business. It's fair to say that Wi-Fi is becoming as essential in the business world as that old standby, a cup of coffee.[7]

Everything Verizon says is true, right? But, the language is generic. It tells you nothing about what the experience will be like working with Verizon to accomplish your goals. Will the people at Verizon take you seriously? Will they care about you?

Now, let's compare this with Sprint's approach. Here's a snapshot from its small business website. It's not just a page but an interactive campaign, including an e-book that tells a story, frame by frame.

The Agile Business Manifesto
How to accelerate growth without losing your soul

Big companies spend fortunes trying to imitate the mojo you already have.

But imitation is as close as they'll ever get.

You have agility.

You're carrying less baggage. You're closer to your customers. You're not bound by dumb processes and legacy systems.

But here's the thing: mojo and agility are fragile things.

Make bad decisions and they're gone.[8]

Sprint cuts right to the heart of what matters to small business owners. It speaks like a person—like someone talking to a friend. The word "manifesto" is inspiring and wakes you up. You feel as though Sprint is truly on your side.

Even a large enterprise like Sprint can define a unique brand personality and be brave enough to break out of the expected corporate mold.

This content-driven campaign achieved a 32% increase in visits to the website within the first month and increased social media traffic more than five times. According to the company's brand monitor survey, people who viewed this campaign were more than twice as likely to consider Sprint for business solutions[9]

Johns Hopkins Medical School

Next, let's look at a smaller organization that wanted to attract students who were the right fit for the school.

Johns Hopkins Medical School was very clear about its goals for a website refresh project. It wanted to make the admissions process more accessible and transparent. It had thousands of applications for 125 slots, which meant fierce competition and an overwhelmed admissions office. It also was battling the lure of Boston-based medical schools and needed to entice students to move to Baltimore. The school wanted prospective students to understand more about the Hopkins experience from the start so those students could self-select. Those who were truly a good cultural fit for the school would apply.

What Hopkins wanted prospective students to say after visiting their site:

- *This place is the cutting edge of medicine. I want to be part of it.*

- *I love the feeling of community at Johns Hopkins, where I will be supported and encouraged to explore my own course of study.*

- *Here is everything I need to know to submit a med school application.*

- *Ooh! I could live in Baltimore.*

This is the text of the Admissions page of the medical school website before the refresh.

> *The Johns Hopkins University School of Medicine is an international leader in the education of physicians and clinical scientists in biomedical research and in the application of medical knowledge in patient care. In addition to its M.D. program, the School of Medicine offers Ph.D. and master's degrees, as well as a combined M.D./PhD.*
>
> *The excitement of discovery and medical innovation is a prime animating force at Johns*

Hopkins. Daily, colleagues come together to explore new ideas and cross-fertilize ongoing research. People come to Johns Hopkins medical facilities from around the world, confident that they will receive the best, most comprehensive, most cost-effective care available anywhere.

Just like the example above involving Verizon, the information on the original Hopkins page isn't wrong. But it's not memorable or distinctive. It doesn't give you a picture of what it would really be like to enroll at Hopkins and it doesn't connect with you emotionally. Additionally, it uses complex and lengthy sentence structure, which makes it difficult for readers to absorb online.

Below is the "after" version of the language used on the updated page.

'The practice of medicine is an art, not a trade; a calling, not a business; a calling in which your heart will be exercised equally with your head.'

—William Osler
John Hopkins founding physician

If medicine is your passion, and your head and heart are aligned in the desire to promote health and expand biomedical knowledge, then the Johns Hopkins University School of Medicine might be for you. Since 1893, we have been dedicated to training the next generation of great medical leaders...Whether your journey brings you to Baltimore next fall or to another medical school, we wish you the best of luck. You have chosen a noble career.

After reading this page, you feel like joining Hopkins makes you part of something larger than yourself. After the launch of the new website, students who applied to Hopkins were better educated about the process of applying to the school and had greater understanding about the Hopkins experience. They didn't require as much direct contact from the overwhelmed admissions office to field questions.[10]

Thycotic

For our third example, let's look at a small cyber security company taking on the 800-pound gorillas in their industry. Thycotic started out as a scrappy underdog and embraced that position. The company culture evolved naturally as collaborative and transparent and the team built those traits into their product experience.

As it grew, Thycotic launched new products and gained market share. Customers liked the agility and control Thycotic's software provided. But Thycotic's website and marketing content were inconsistent with its culture and values. The language and visual imagery didn't paint an authentic picture of the innovative, authoritative leader the company had become or the benefits it provided for customers.

Thycotic had grown so fast that it never really invested in defining its brand personality, at least not in terms of a formal marketing process. As a result, competitors crafted their own characterization of the company as a bit player—in essence, defining Thycotic's brand personality while it was looking the other way.

Below is a screenshot of Thycotic's previous homepage.

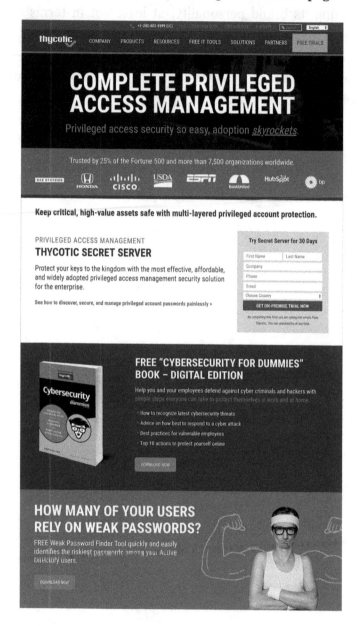

After going through the brand personality development process we'll walk through in the subsequent chapters, Thycotic is now able to tell its story in a way that truly reflects its culture and mission, with focused messaging that clarifies its competitive advantages. The company has embraced its role as an industry leader and takes on competitors with a unique point of view and inspiring language.

Here is the updated homepage to compare.

The year of the brand personality rollout, Thycotic's enterprise sales more than doubled, outpacing the market by 2 1/2 times. Website conversion rates reached 7%. For a deeper dive into the Thycotic story, you can read the full case study at www.centerboard-marketing.com/thycotic.

Throughout this book we'll look at many more real-life examples that demonstrate how a strong brand personality can help you accomplish your business goals. You'll hear stories of companies that improved organizational alignment, accelerated sales, gained market share and bested the competition.

What we covered:

- Clarify your goals at the start of your brand project.

- Determine what you're hoping to gain from defining or enhancing your brand personality.

- Define how you'll measure success.

What's next:

- How to build a brand SWAT team and plan for your brand personality launch by starting with the end in mind.

CHAPTER 2
PLANNING

What you'll learn: *Planning decisions you make at this stage impact your success down the line. In this chapter we'll talk about how to set up your brand SWAT team and key considerations for scope and timeline.*

Fewer than 50% of employees believe in their own company's brand idea. Even less say they are able to execute on it.[11] What makes people so unprepared or, depending on your perspective, so cynical? Here's what I think.

Many people have been through a brand project before in their careers and haven't seen results, either because the brand definition didn't hit the mark or because it was poorly, inconsistently executed. As we've discussed, when brand projects consist only of high-level visions and taglines they get diluted when a team on the ground attempts to build content or campaigns.

One common misstep organizations make is to keep the brand project hidden away until they're ready for a big reveal. When brand discussions are conducted only by executives behind closed doors, they lack perspective and buy-in from the rest of the organization. Then, when the organization receives the news that there is a "new" brand, it's no wonder they don't embrace it. Worse, because the brand was defined without incorporating multiple perspectives, it's incomplete and likely inaccurate.

That's why this planning stage is essential.

First, put together your brand SWAT team

One of the first decisions to make is who to include on your core brand team. These are the folks with ultimate responsibility for the planning and execution of the brand personality. The size and makeup of a brand team varies by organization, but there are a few key roles that every brand team needs:

Brand guardian

The brand guardian is typically an internal marketing leader, often responsible for rallying the troops. He or she will have an understanding of brand touchpoints and the marketing execution process. The guardian may be supported by other members of the marketing team with specific expertise.

Sales leader

In many organizations marketing and sales are like oil and water. The best way to build alignment is to include the sales perspective from the start of a brand project. Include at least one sales leader who can gather and consolidate perspectives from the larger sales team. The salespeople on the SWAT team should also be able to envision brand touchpoints beyond the sales process.

Human Resources

This person knows your organization inside and out and can provide a reality check to make sure the brand personality reflects your organization's culture and values.

Product managers and product marketing managers

They help link the high-level, umbrella messages that express your overall corporate culture and your values with the specific capabilities your products and services have— features that provide the most value and can set your offerings apart in customers' minds.

Project manager

The project manager keeps the team on track and moving toward the launch date. Particularly as you move from the brand personality development process toward execution and launch stages, the project manager will ensure all the moving pieces stay coordinated.

Executive sponsor

A member of your organization's leadership team should be involved in the process. This person doesn't necessarily need to be involved in every detail or attend every meeting, but he or she must be on hand for major decisions. As we go through the brand personality development process, I'll identify areas where many organizations struggle with potential conflicts and even controversies that benefit from the involvement of an executive decision maker.

External expert/facilitator

Most brand projects find that an external strategist is helpful to guide the team along the brand development process and provide a much-needed external perspective. Often, internal teams struggle with seeing their own brand from a customer or competitive point of view. An external person can ask questions of customers and competitors that an internal team can't. This person can shine a light on areas of potential conflict or gaps and make sure they're resolved before they cause roadblocks.

Involve employees from the beginning.

"A brand positioning that best motivates the team, that they can deliver, is the only one that will really work."

—Forbes[12]

Don't hide your brand team's work. The more you involve folks from different areas of your organization, the more committed they'll be to the consistent execution of the brand personality when you're ready for launch.

Beyond the core team, you may choose to have other people involved throughout the process or bring them in at different points to gather their input or feedback. Other team members can include content creators such as writers and designers, as well as other people who have direct relationships with prospects and customers, such as customer service or technical support. We'll talk more about the importance of these supplemental team members in Chapter 7.

Plan ahead for your rollout.

It may feel like we're jumping ahead to think about the rollout now. But in my experience, it's better to start with the end in mind. You'll want to give your team sufficient time to plan and execute your new brand personality. By setting a target launch date now, you'll keep everyone moving toward the same goal and keep them accountable for their part in the process.

Set a date and work backward. I've worked with companies that keep a common calendar on a wall and strike through each day as they move toward their target date.

To choose a realistic date, think about scale. There are different levels of brand rollouts and each has pros and cons. Which path you choose will depend on a number of factors, including size of your organization, your budget and resources, and timing constraints.

Brand "relaunch" vs. brand "refresh"— choose the model that's right for you

Brand "relaunch" model

In this model, everything new goes live at once. The goal is to update all physical and digital brand touchpoints, including your website, print collateral, email, social media, event signage and booth, sales presentations and more before you can flip the switch on the new brand.

Many companies choose an industry event or schedule an event of their own (or a Super Bowl commercial if you have gobs of cash) for the big reveal.

Pros:

- Brand personality is consistent across all touchpoints.

- Opportunity to clear out ineffective or outdated materials.

- Employees and customers consider the brand change a major milestone.

Cons:

- Lots of moving pieces must be coordinated.

- Big hit to your budget in a short amount of time.

- Time pressure can be stressful for your team.

Brand "refresh" model

Instead of preparing everything to launch simultaneously, some companies find it more manageable to roll out a brand personality in phases. To do this you'd pick high-visibility, high-priority touchpoints and update them first, followed by the next wave and so on. Perhaps that means key pages on your website and your sales presentation get the most attention in wave one.

From a certain point forward, any new sales, marketing and product materials would reflect the new brand personality. Older content would get phased out naturally, as it reaches the end of its lifecycle.

If the brand personality you define departs radically from the current language and design your customers experience, the refresh model can be tricky to execute. It will be important to design the look and feel as well as the language of any new content so that it advances your new brand personality while blending with the old.

In the refresh model, old branding elements can linger for way too long if you don't set a firm end date for them. Consider AMTRAK's arrow logo from the 1970's, which still graces some train stations and road signs today, almost two decades after being replaced with a new logo.[13]

Pros:

- Allows you to spread budget and resources out over longer period of time.

- Gives you a chance to test and refine brand while it rolls out.

Cons:

- Tricky to blend old with the new without disrupting the brand experience.

- Subtle changes may not make the impact you need.

- Inconsistencies may confuse or frustrate employees or customers.

STORY FROM THE TRENCHES

One of Centerboard's professional services clients chose the relaunch path. Every marketing asset—from the website to product collateral to email templates and social media—changed the same day.

The company launched the new brand internally at an all-hands meeting with several hundred people attending. The CMO stood in front of the company and told them it was time to "burn the boats." He shared this story:

> *"In 1519 Hernán Cortés led an expedition of 600 Spaniards, 16 horses and 11 boats to Mexico to capture an island. Upon arrival, Cortés ordered his men to burn their boats. This sent a clear message: There is no turning back."*

To translate this parable into brand terms, he told the sales team in no uncertain terms that older materials should no longer be used. They combed their company Intranet, Dropbox, wiki and other places where people had old materials squirrelled away and replaced them with new.

Within three months after the brand relaunch, this company more than doubled its lead conversion rate.

Create a brand touchpoint worksheet

Map everywhere people can experience your brand. Put all of these brand touchpoints on your project plan. Once you define your brand personality you'll review each touchpoint to assess how well it reflects the traits and messages you want to convey. Then you'll update them to match.

Important: Assign an internal owner to each category and, if necessary, to each named touchpoint. Without an owner, a project is unlikely to be completed. Assign timelines for each touchpoint depending on which rollout model you use.

Your brand worksheet will look something like this:

Worksheet: Brand Touchpoints

BRAND TOUCHPOINT	LAUNCH DATE	OWNER	COST
Website Key webpages Online chat			
Emails E-newsletter Sales emails Customer service emails			
Advertisements Digital ads Print ads			
Social media descriptions LinkedIn Twitter Facebook			
Presentations Sales pitch deck Product presentations Event presentations			
Event booth and signage			
PR boilerplate			
Collateral Brochures Product sheets White papers Infographics Videos and interactive tools			
Partner/reseller materials			
Third-party websites			
Store signage			
Experiential marketing			
Office locations			
Your product interface, error messages and micro-text			

Consistency matters

The strongest brands are consistent across every touchpoint. Your brand personality guides the stories you choose to tell as well as the channels you select to go to market.

Anna Pickard, the editorial director at Slack known for stewarding the brand's distinctive personality, describes the importance of consistency this way:

> *"There's a sense of recognition. The same simple, straightforward language that helps you in the onboarding process is the one that carries you through every interaction ... throughout, it should feel like nothing more than a person, talking to another person. Human to human."*[14]

You can't change a brand personality like you're changing shoes. Let's say you have a cluttered, difficult-to-navigate website full of jargon and complex sentences. Pasting a tagline on top that says you're "The Easy Way to Get the Job Done" isn't going to change customers' opinions of you. Your customers will call you on it.

What we covered:

- Spin up your brand SWAT team.

- Determine your rollout model.

- List brand touchpoints for evaluation and updates.

What's next:

- Put in place the three critical building blocks to a brand personality.

CHAPTER 3
BUILDING BLOCKS

What you'll learn: In this chapter you'll learn the three building blocks that secure your brand personality on a solid foundation. You'll also find sets of questions you must ask of your company and your customers as well as hands-on activities to drive prioritization and consensus.

"Mask the logo on your site. Do you sound different, unique—like yourself? Or do you sound like everyone else ... including your competitors? Said another way: If the label fell off ... would people know it was you?"

– Ann Handley
author of *Everybody Writes*[15]

Your brand personality is simply an external expression of your company's unique story. It's the humanity behind your business. You want people to read something that comes from your company and say, without knowing the source: *"Hey: that sounds like xxx."*

To craft a powerful, differentiated brand personality, you must know three things:

1. Which core values and behaviors drive your culture and goals.

2. Who your target customers are and what they care about most.

3. How what you do is different from (and hopefully better than) your competition.

It's much, much more effective to nourish and communicate a brand personality after you answer these fundamental questions. In fact, it's next to impossible to construct a brand out of thin air for a company that hasn't gone through this exploration.

If you aren't authentic, your attempt to build a brand personality will backfire

The goal of defining your brand personality isn't to turn you into something you're not. It's not about following the latest fad.

For example, many tech companies are trying to adopt funny, quirky personas to seem "cool." That doesn't mean you have to do the same if that isn't who you are. A marketing agency or summer intern can create a funny, funky website or social media feed, but if the rest of your organization can't sustain this style, it will fail.

It's actually dangerous to prop up a false brand personality. If you set false expectations in your marketing materials, you'll have to start from scratch when developing a relationship with customers based on who you truly are. It's like using someone else's photo for your dating profile, only to disappoint once you meet in person.

You may not describe yourself perfectly. The only caveat is that you have to be honest.

It can be difficult for an internal team to articulate its own brand personality. Internal teams often spend time with similar colleagues and customers who appreciate them. They can have trouble taking a wider view of how their brand compares to competitors' or is perceived by potential buyers.

Take this famous fable as an example. In *The Blind Men and the Elephant*, six travelers came across an elephant. "My, it's very like a wall," said one man who only felt the side. "My, it's very like a snake," described another who was holding the trunk. In the same way each man created his own version of reality, each person within an organization often has a limited view of what's important and what makes the company special, based on his or her own experiences.

When I work with organizations to define their brand personality, I focus first on understanding their story. That requires gathering and analyzing information from multiple people within the company, customers and competitors. It's only by bringing different viewpoints together and combining them with external perspectives that an authentic brand personality emerges.

STORY FROM THE TRENCHES

Mailchimp, known for its distinctive, playful brand personality, recently redesigned its branding elements. It updated its logo, wordmark, typeface, colors and imagery. But while Mailchimp freshened its look and feel, its core brand personality remained faithful to the company's fundamental values.

Gene Lee, Mailchimp's VP of design, explains:

> *"We want to show our customers that being yourself is good for business by providing the tools and confidence to take risks, especially as their businesses evolve. We champion authenticity, originality and expressiveness because it's what helps us—and our customers— stand out. We hope to inspire them to be more bold and creative in their own branding efforts."*

Changing your colors doesn't mean changing your personality.

Mailchimp can incorporate a wry sense of humor that few other companies can pull off because it mirrors its goals and values. It doesn't matter whether it does so in blue or in yellow.[16]

Let's break each of the three building blocks down, one by one.

CULTURE, CORE VALUES AND BEHAVIORS

Your brand personality should reflect your company's culture, including the values and behaviors of your leadership and employees.

> *"All of the actions of authentic brands are born from and aligned with their core purpose. They are deeply in touch with why they do what they do, and for this reason they're perceived radically different than their competitors. Even if their service offerings are essentially the same, the purpose behind those services is as distinct as a fingerprint."*
>
> – Brian Lischer
> CEO of Ignyte[17]

Many companies think about culture as something that impacts how employees feel about coming to work. For many of us, it's important to work for a company that reflects our personal beliefs and priorities. This doesn't mean the company needs to have a purely altruistic mission, however; even a company that makes gobs of money selling widgets can have values that drive choices and interactions.

How would you describe your company culture?

If you aren't sure of the answer, ask yourself and others around the company these questions:

- *Was there a higher purpose or aspirational goal when the company was founded? Has it changed?*

- *Why do you love working for this organization?*

- *What qualities make an employee successful at your company?*

- *What traits do you seek in a new hire?*

- *How do decisions at your company get made?*

Include different groups and functional areas in your survey of people around the company. Certainly people aren't expected to share all of the same opinions but there almost definitely will be some commonality among the top answers.

Ask leaders in your company questions that encourage them to share their unique perspectives. I like to ask subject matter experts that I interview, *"What would most people disagree with you about?"* This is a great question to uncover their points of view and test their comfort level with sharing provocative opinions. You'll find many more questions to ask in your *Brand Breakthrough Action Guide.*

Bring areas of conflict out into the open

Brand development is a journey of self-discovery and requires making difficult choices. "The fastest way to a 'vanilla' brand is to try to please everyone," warns Cameron Caswell, Senior Manager, Content and Brand Marketing at Synopsys.[18]

It's healthy to dig up some controversy during this stage and bring areas of disagreement or inconsistency into the light so they can be addressed. A skilled facilitator can identify areas of conflict and work with an organization to resolve them, rather than leaving them to fester.

For example, I worked recently with a company that provided both marketing *services* (strategy and hands-on execution support) as well as *products* (proprietary algorithms and technology for programmatic advertising) to e-commerce companies. Many of the company leaders felt the brand personality should prioritize the service aspect of the company culture and showcase the business' role as a supportive, flexible advisor. Others wanted to emphasize technical prowess and product innovation in the brand personality. Both sides of the coin can be woven into a brand personality, but only one side can take the primary role.

A debate like this can derail your brand development work if you don't bring it to conclusion. If people within an organization express radically different views of their values or culture, those discrepancies will become more difficult to iron out as you progress in defining a brand personality. If you don't force prioritization and make hard choices, the discrepancies will damage your brand in the long run.

In the end, the CEO convinced the team to prioritize the "technical prowess" aspect of the company's brand personality in order to attract investors as well as customers. Perhaps not everyone agreed, but after making the hard choice, the team was able to move on to the next phase with its priorities in place.

Hands-on Activity: Brand Pyramid

Gather a cross-section of people from around the company to make sure you have multiple perspectives represented. Give yourselves some physical space and head space.

Draw a pyramid on the wall, divided into three sections from bottom to top: Core, Defining, and Differentiating.

Think of these levels as similar to Maslow's hierarchy of needs, which categorizes human needs into five levels that progress from the most basic to the most "actualized."[19]

- "Core" refers to any characteristic of your organization that's fundamental to what you do. Restaurant? You serve food. Watchmaker? Your product tells time.

- The next level up is "Defining." Now you get into the benefits you offer and the nuances of the features and functions you provide.

- Finally, you reach the pinnacle, "Differentiating." Here you fill in the characteristics that make you special among all other similar organizations. To graduate from Defining to Differentiating, a characteristic has to be *so* unique, a benefit *so* exceptional, that none of your competitors could say the same.

Next, set out a selection of pre-written words that describe attributes and behaviors related to your company culture. You can use colorful Post-it notes for this. The set I create is customized based on interviews with staff, customers, marketing materials and SEO/keyword research. They're an educated guess as to words that an organization would use when describing itself.

Have the group discuss each word in turn, evaluating the degree to which it represents the organization and to which of the three levels it belongs. Some words will be easy. Others will be more controversial.

You'll find people will stand up and move words around, and they'll even list new words as they discuss the pros and cons.

You can have people vote, but be sure to force them to prioritize. Again, the role of the facilitator is to point out conflicts (you can't be both modern and traditional at the same time) and force difficult choices.

Why does this work?

This isn't simply arts and crafts. It's a tactile experience that gets people out of their chairs and engaged in creating something together. The goal is to facilitate debate in a constructive way so that brand creation is more transparent and incorporates ideas from multiple people.

As a result, the words you choose to describe your organization are more likely to reflect its authentic qualities and more likely to stick.

After the exercise, your pyramid will look something like this:

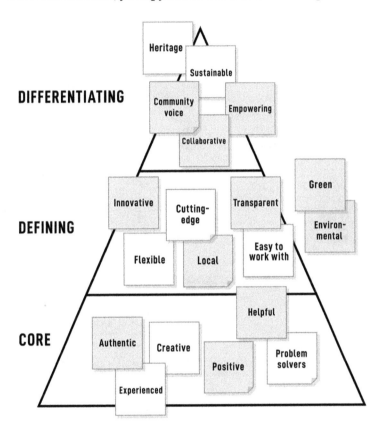

When putting this group together, consider if you should hold one session or more. In some organizations staff may not feel comfortable sharing opinions about company culture when their managers are in the room—but you still want to include their insights. Make sure you include people who have direct connections to customers and people who have worked in other organizations during their careers.

STORY FROM THE TRENCHES

Maggie Whittier is director of content strategy at ARMATURE Solutions Corporation and was previously director of content at creative agency RepEquity.

She shares her advice on facilitating brand workshops:

> *Be forewarned: You may meet resistance from some people and you'll have to win them over. I once walked into a room to start a brand workshop for a conservative financial institution and faced a row of senior execs sitting with their arms crossed. They were told to be there but they clearly didn't want to be there and they didn't believe in the process.*
>
> *In some companies, marketing—especially branding—isn't taken seriously by the rest of the organization. People think it's all buzzwords and fluff. And, to be honest, sometimes marketers are to blame for this perception because they don't understand enough about the products or how the business works to move beyond high-level branding statements to more nuanced, detailed positioning.*
>
> *Marketers have to be willing to go deeper and be more specific, focusing on what's authentic, true and awesome about the brand—even if it's not the most exciting thing in the world. I'll take a single small, true quality over hyperbolic blather any day.*

To overcome resistance, you need to show people why brand matters for their job, in their day-to-day work, to achieve their goals. Your brand positioning and mission statements serve as your North Star, but you can (and should) bring these principles down to earth so that people can act on them.

Translate the ideas and connect the dots. Talk to salespeople about how their pitch deck could be different from everyone else's. Talk to HR folks about how a fresh way of crafting job descriptions and training materials can influence the quality of candidates. Show customer service reps how the words and tone they use can change customer perceptions. All of these small daily actions reinforce the brand identity, and when everyone understands and believes in the brand framework you've established, the whole is always greater than the sum of the parts.

As for the finance guys? I presented them with three positioning statements and three mission statements and highlighted keywords in each for discussion. I explained my rationale for the words in red—this word was inspired by a story that one of your customers told me, and that word came up a lot in the online forums—and they perked right up. Before I knew it, they were picking favorites and debating over the words, and I knew they were on board.[20]

BUILDING BLOCK 2:
TARGET CUSTOMERS

Many brand personality projects stop at describing the company culture. But your brand personality isn't as simple as saying your company is "innovative" or "friendly" or "open." Words like these don't provide enough guidance to create a fully formed personality for your brand.

> *"Your brand is what people say about you when you aren't in the room."*
>
> —Jeff Bezos
> founder and CEO of Amazon

Dig deeper. Look from the outside in.

The next step is to turn the description of your company culture around to an external view. How is your company culture experienced by your *customers?* This is sometimes referred to as "inside-out branding."

Consider how customers interact with your brand at every stage of the buying cycle:

Attracting prospects

People judge you based on first impressions, before they have a chance to meet you. Having a strong brand personality makes it easier to attract customers who are a good fit for your company. As you're growing your company, it's tempting to try and be all things to all people. But turning yourself inside out for anyone willing to pay is exhausting and unproductive. Instead of trying to be a chameleon, if you put forth a unique and authentic brand personality, customers will begin to self-select. They'll say, "This company aligns with my personality and my values." And they'll come to you.

Convincing buyers

As customers interact with people inside your organization, demonstrating a consistent brand personality builds trust. Buyers know what they're going to get with you. Their experience doesn't feel like a bait-and-switch tactic, where they're promised one thing and receive another.

Retaining and referring customers

Having a defined brand personality makes it easier for customers who like working with you to tell others about you. You don't want to make your customers work hard to promote your brand. Instead, give them the tools they need to do it.

How you *want* customers to feel about your brand may not be how they *actually* feel

It's critical to the brand development process that you get an unbiased view of your company from a customer perspective. Lori Worth from PR firm Vibe Communications puts it this way: "You can say that your company logo stands for X, but what if people's experience with your brand actually equals Y? Then, like it or not, your brand perception is Y."[21]

In the expression of your brand, you need to meet your customers where they are, not push your agenda ahead of their needs. The more clearly you understand your customers' challenges, goals, feelings and experiences, the stronger your brand will resonate with them.

Here's an example from Target. An internal training document encouraged employees to emphasize "fast, casual, direct and high-tech" communication to connect with millennials. Sounds like a good idea, but then Target started tweeting using hashtags, #yolo, #bae and #onfleek in an awkward attempt to sound cool.[22]

"When you see a brand aging down its social channels it's a warning sign in most cases that the brand is struggling to connect in a meaningful way with its audience," says Shankar Gupta, vice president of strategy at 360i about the Target misstep. "If you can't understand your audience well enough to develop a genuine connection, it's an all-too-tempting shortcut to dress up your advertising with youthful slang to create a superficial connection."[23]

The key is understanding your target audience. If you're a brand like Chubbies or Taco Bell, known for a youthful or hip personality, you can use the word "bae." But if you're Applebee's or Quaker Oats, throwing in a few hashtags won't help you suddenly get invited to the cool kids' table.

Who says brands have to please everyone? Your goal is to connect with the people who matter to you.

It's time to talk to your customers

If possible, talk with prospective customers who are considering working with you, happy current customers, unhappy current customers and prior customers or prospects who chose a different solution. Direct conversations are the best way to start because they allow you to follow customers' lead and pivot a conversation to the areas of most importance to them. Talk with them about the decisions they make throughout the buying process and their interactions with you at every step.

An unbiased third party can often have more candid conversations about customer perceptions and uncover pain points you haven't heard before.

Don't simply ask your customers about the vendors they choose to solve their immediate problems. Listen for trends that customers are concerned about, both for the short term and the long run. What's happening economically, politically, legally, technologically and culturally that keeps them up at night?

Build a listening post for broader feedback

Of course, you won't be able to talk with all your customers. Some brands have hundreds of thousands of customers or more and can't count on having representative conversations.

To capture a wider net of customer conversations, build a "listening post." Set up Google Alerts. Follow industry leaders, competitors, partners, analysts and key hashtags on social media. Subscribe to industry publications and product review sites. Tune into conversations on community sites, forums and Slack channels.

Social listening tools can help you track and analyze the topics they discuss and the sentiments they share.

Develop empathy for your customers

After researching your customers, there are a few big questions you should be able to answer:

- *What triggers them to find a solution like yours?*

- *What challenges does your organization help solve for them?*

- *Why would they decide to work with your company or use your products specifically?*

- *How does working with your organization help them meet their personal goals as well as their business ones?*

- *What do they expect from your brand in the long term?*

- *This is my favorite question to ask: How would they solve their problems if your organization did not exist?*

In seeking answers to these questions, you're not just looking for the rational, measurable benefits your customers get from your products and services. You're also listening for clues about their emotions.

When you make an emotional connection, you build trust and loyalty. Customers with an emotional connection are three times more likely to recommend you and three times likelier to repurchase. They're also less price sensitive and less likely to shop around.[24]

To create a compelling brand personality that connects with your customers on a deep, emotional level, you must understand:

- *How do most customers feel when they first start working with you? Are they frustrated at their current situation? Worried about the future?*

- *How do they feel after interacting with your people or your products? Excited? Energized? Empowered?*

- *How can you help them change the way they feel?*

Hearing the words and the tone customers use to answer these questions helps get inside their heads and their hearts.

Hands-on Activity: Emotional Goals

Create a list of things you want your customers to feel. Here are some words to get you started:

Brave	Empowered	Safe
Wise	Triumphant	Rebellious
Strong	Delighted	Inspired
Protected	Healthy	Competitive
Confident	Connected	Optimistic
Cool	Amused	Energized
Lighthearted	Unique	Comfortable
Relieved	Nurtured	Hopeful

You can capture and rank these emotions through a survey or in a discussion format as in the pyramid activity. Prioritize the top three to four emotions you'd like customers to experience. Root out areas of potential inconsistency. For example, it's hard to feel comfortable and rebellious at the same time.

Now, check this list against what your customers told you is most important to them. Find those areas of overlap to make sure your goals ring true with your customers' needs.

STORY FROM THE TRENCHES

Lauren Lucchese is the head of AI content at Capital One. She is also a mentor at Designation, a UX bootcamp, and co-organizer of Chicago's UX Strategy Meetup.

The following is excerpted from an interview conducted by content strategist Vinish Garg and published on Medium:

> "At Capital One, content design means using language to create meaningful, personal interactions with customers across all touchpoints of an experience. Content designers use words to drive emotion, knowing that our choices can make or break the entire user experience if we're not careful. Essentially, we are experience designers. It's just that instead of visual elements, our main tool is words.
>
> By focusing on the words we're using right out the gate, we can ensure that we're answering the right customer questions and providing the right information when they need it most, before anyone starts prototyping or creating higher-fidelity designs.
>
> Empathy has EVERYTHING to do with how our team shows up, both in the experiences we design for our customers and in the interactions we have with each other as the people responsible for creating these experiences.

Research provides us with a deeper level of understanding when it comes to our customers and the problems we want to solve, for them and for the company. Without it, we're making decisions based on our own assumptions and best guesses, which is obviously never ideal.

When we get it right, we demonstrate that we have our customers' best interests at heart. It helps them believe that we care about them, because we do.

Understandable, meaningful, tailored experiences that feel like personalized conversations foster loyalty, which can have a significant ROI for the business, especially as customers mature. Loyalty is much harder to measure in the short term, but will prove invaluable for those companies visionary enough to play the long game."[25]

I love the part about creating empathy for customers. My favorite line from this post is, "when we get it right, we demonstrate that we have our customers' best interests at heart. It helps them believe that we care about them, because we do."

Lauren's perspective reinforces that your messaging can't only be about what *you* want to express. If you keep your customers' needs front and center, you'll be able to craft formidable messaging with the power to convince and convert.

BUILDING BLOCK 3:
COMPETITION

No matter how innovative or disruptive your offering, never assume there's no one else out there doing what you do. There's always a competitor. Even if no one does what you're doing today, someone is surely thinking about it.

The biggest competitor you're up against? Status quo. What are your customers doing today to solve their challenges? Are they using another vendor? Are they building something themselves? Are they attempting to use a similar product or service to fill *most* of their needs, assuming there is no other option? Those are competitors too.

Explore the ways top competitors present their brand personality to customers by reviewing competitive websites, content, social feeds and presentations. If possible, you even may do some "secret shopping" by chat or phone to see how they interact with sales prospects.

Review marketing messages they emphasize. What aspects of their products, services or company story do they prioritize in their content marketing and sales process? What promises do they make? Do their customers believe they keep those promises?

What are you looking for?

You're looking for patterns of similarity and gaps or weaknesses among competitors that provide opportunities for radical differentiation.

What stories are your competitors NOT telling which you believe customers need to know? Is this a market filled with conservative, old-school players? Maybe it's ready for a new voice that stands out from the crowd. Or is the market filled with low priced upstarts and you believe your role is to stand firm on tradition and quality?

Even if you compete in a crowded market full of similar alternatives, your approach, history, pricing—something!—must make you unique.

When you find a gap, lean into it.

The answer will make you stand out among competitors as long as it resonates with your customers and feels authentic to your organization.

Worksheet: Value Drivers

Take all the things customers say are critical and list them as "value drivers." These could be strategic goals, pain points, purchase criteria or success metrics. Prioritize value drivers by importance and percentage of customers that cared about each issue.

Next, plot your brand and competitors on the chart. Honestly assess whether you and your competitors sufficiently address each value driver.

In the example below, strategic goal "b" is something customers care about AND it's something your brand addresses, but your competitors don't. Bingo! Lean into that value driver in your conversations and content.

CUSTOMER VALUE DRIVERS	YOUR BRAND	COMPETITOR A	COMPETITOR B
Strategic goals			
a.		X	X
b.	X		
Pain points			
a.	X	X	X
b.	X	X	X
Purchase criteria			
a.	X	X	
b.	X		X
Success metrics			
a.			X
b.		X	

In the following chapters we'll return to these three building blocks and demonstrate how they create the foundation of your messaging architecture and support a powerful brand personality.

What we covered:

- Recognize and prioritize traits that define your company culture, values and behaviors.

- Understand what makes your customers tick and empathize with their challenges and goals.

- Clarify what makes your company unique among competitors.

What's next:

- Put on your hard hat. This next chapter is where we really start building. We start by viewing your organization through the lens of a brand archetype.

CHAPTER 4
CHOOSE YOUR BRAND ARCHETYPE

What you'll learn: In this chapter you'll meet brand personalities based on classic "archetypes." You'll understand how they reflect different character traits and convey messages through their language choices.

Archetypes are a concept named by Swiss psychologist Carl Jung[26], but they have existed since humans first started telling stories. These iconic characters appear throughout literature and embody specific personality traits and behaviors.

The benefit of using archetypes as a mirror for your brand personality is to anchor your brand against concepts that are already known to your audience, in fact embedded within their subconscious.

There are dozens of archetypes from which to choose. I typically work with a set of six common archetypes that can be differentiated easily in order to clarify and confirm a company's brand personality. These six have stood the test of time and translate well across generations. They can apply to both B2B and B2C brands.

Below are key elements of each archetype and real-life examples of organizations that have adopted them as their brand personality. Pay special attention to their language choices and the emotions they evoke.

THE PIONEER

First to do something and optimistic about the future

The key element of The Pioneer is the emphasis on being "first." He's an innovator and a trailblazer, unafraid to explore and discover new territories and expand a customer's vision of the future. The Pioneer makes customers feel energized, optimistic and unique. Let's look at some Pioneer brands in action.

Levi's

The team behind Levi's "Go Forth" campaign looked to the company's origins to reflect the core brand personality.

> *"The men who had set out for the gold hiding in the uncharted lands of California during the famous Gold Rush of 1849 were known as the 49ers, and they had taken a big gamble, often risking life or*

death, to try to strike it rich. We had to tell the story in a way that would ignite a newfound interest in the hearts and minds of new consumers. We asked ourselves, 'Who are our modern-day pioneers?' We wanted to find people who were embodying that spirit of progress and hard work and pull them into a new conversation, one that celebrated their sense of craft, of making things, of the integrity that comes from doing that kind of work well.

"When we said 'pioneer,' we weren't thinking of a grizzled old prospector chewing tobacco and swilling whiskey. We were imagining today's artists, craftspeople, designers, teachers and builders. When we said, 'Go Forth,' we knew we were looking for the spirit of adventure and discovery we wanted people to feel when they interacted with the brand."[27]

Red Bull

Red Bull built its reputation on a series of firsts. It created a new category of beverages—the energy drink. It was an early adopter of content marketing, using content to build passionate advocates of the brand. Rather than take the common path of sponsoring events, Red Bull created its own sporting events and festivals. Rather than simply buy television ads, it was among the first to leverage the power of YouTube as a content medium.

Red Bull makes people feel they could be pioneers as well. When customers see athletes performing incredible feats they feel inspired to push themselves to new heights. Consider these lines from some of Red Bull's commercials: "The only limit is the one you set yourself." And, "You can dream about it or you can go out and make it happen."[28]

THE REBEL

Aggressively undoing wrongs, often controversial or counterculture

Similar to The Pioneer, The Rebel forges a non-traditional path. But his manner is more aggressive and his perspective more radical. In taking on the status quo, The Rebel relishes a challenge. He's willing to shake things up to get results. The Rebel makes customers feel brave, strong, competitive and triumphant. Below are some Rebel brands in action.

Virgin Atlantic

Virgin Atlantic prides itself on bringing travelers new experiences. Consider the language of the 2013 campaign, "Flying in the Face of Ordinary."[29] Or, banner text on the Virgin website in 2018, which urges you to "Depart the everyday."[30]

The Marketing Society describes the origins of Virgin's brand personality and how it has maintained consistency over the years.

"The brand voice was modeled on the personality of Virgin's founder, Richard Branson. If the Virgin Atlantic brand can be said to have attitude, that attitude was his—maverick, challenging, witty and innovative. The consistency in Virgin Atlantic communications came from the cultivation of a distinctive brand voice and stylish visual identity. Whether launching a new route in the network, communicating the onboard experience or taking tactical advantage of a gaff by long-term rival British Airways (BA), this distinctive Virgin Atlantic attitude was fundamental to the communications strategy."[31]

Warby Parker

Warby Parker took on the established eyewear industry. It unraveled the annoying and expensive process of ordering eyeglasses, built its own supply chain and gave consumers more purchasing power. The company is currently valued at $175 billion.[32]

From the Warby Parker website:

Warby Parker was founded with a rebellious spirit and a lofty objective: to offer designer eyewear at a revolutionary price, while leading the way for socially conscious businesses.

Every idea starts with a problem. Ours was simple: glasses are too expensive. We were students when one of us lost his glasses on a backpacking trip. The cost of replacing them was so high that he spent the first semester of grad school without them, squinting and complaining. (We don't recommend this.) The rest of us had similar experiences, and we were amazed at how hard it was to find a pair of great frames that didn't leave our wallets bare. Where were the options?

It turns out there was a simple explanation. The eyewear industry is dominated by a single company that has been able to keep prices artificially high while reaping huge profits from consumers who have no other options.

We started Warby Parker to create an alternative.[33]

Instructure

In the online education industry, upstart Instructure took on established players such as Blackboard with a simple, cost-efficient solution. Instead of bogging a learning management system down with complex capabilities, Instructure built a streamlined product that focused only on the most used, most essential features. By 2018, Instructure surpassed Blackboard in market share in what industry analysts call "a stunning development for a company that seemed to have established an unbreakable market dominance a decade ago."[34]

From the company's website:

> *Canvas isn't just a product. It's a breath of fresh air. It's an educational revolution. It's a powerful new way to – pardon our optimism – change the world. It's a rapidly growing company with an industry-pushing platform, 1,100 talented employees, and millions of passionate students and teachers. And, sure, there's also a pretty incredible product in there too.*[35]

THE JESTER

Whimsical, playful and quirky

The Jester is fun-loving and has a quirky or wry sense of humor. He often pokes fun at situations to lighten the mood and can make people laugh at their own foibles. While The Jester can be silly, his humor is always intended to make a point and engage customers so they pay attention and remember what he has to say. The Jester makes customers feel amused, delighted, lighthearted and surprised. Below are some examples of Jester brands.

Ben & Jerry's

Quick with a joke, Ben & Jerry's is all about the happiness great ice cream can bring. The quirky nature of the company's founders is infused within its marketing language and has built a dedicated following among ice cream fans. The brand personality is clear in a Ben & Jerry's store, throughout the company's online presence and in the naming of its products.

"The Tonight Dough," "Cherry Garcia," and "The Americone Dream" are fan favorites.

To build some buzz around new flavors, one of Ben & Jerry's many online quizzes invites people to test out new flavors:

> *You're in the mood for a light, sweet, and utterly euphoric Moo-phoria light ice cream flavor, but as you stand in front of the grocery store freezer, you're awed by the sheer number of choices. Chocolate, caramel, peanut butter, mint—it's overwhelming! Take the quiz below to find your Moo-phoria light ice cream soulmate and skip the freezer fatigue.*[36]

MOO

Business card company Moo stands out in an industry with dozens of competitors selling similar products. Moo uses language and imagery to present an engaging experience from the time customers initiate an order through the confirmation and tracking emails they receive.

"Call it loyalty, call it love, but many of MOO's customers greet even the most mundane interactions, like confirmation emails, with glee, forwarding them to friends and tweeting out quotes," says Margot Bloomstein, content strategist, principal of Appropriate, Inc. and creator of BrandSort, in her review of the MOO brand.[37]

THE GUIDE

Experienced, confident leader and trusted advisor

The Guide is a knowledgeable, indispensable companion. He exercises leadership by example and works shoulder-to-shoulder with customers without losing perspective on the long-term goal. He explores options with customers and helps them navigate the best course. The Guide makes customers feel empowered, confident, wise, healthy and connected. Brands based on The Guide include:

Weight Watchers

Weight Watchers says its proven formula is the way to reach weight loss goals. There's no greater guide than Weight Watcher's spokesperson Oprah Winfrey, who shares her own success with the program and leads others along the same path.

The Weight Watchers home page tells visitors, "Because we've been there. Because we understand. Because it works."[38]

Invision

Invision gives designers the tools and support they need to achieve their goals. Not only does Invision provide software to design and optimize websites and other digital content, the company also has one of the most-followed blogs in the UX and design space.

Invision's core values are front and center on the corporate website, starting with, "Question Assumptions: True innovation and problem solving call us to question everything, even our own bias."[39]

Synopsys

Services companies are often a good fit for The Guide personality as they want to be viewed as experts and trusted advisors. For example, cyber security company (and Centerboard client) Synopsys helps companies build security into their products. Synopsys offers strategic guidance and conducts security testing. Synopsys embraces The Guide personality by designing its marketing materials with an "adventure" theme, emphasizing The Guide's role in taking on challenges and leading the way to success.

From the Synopsys *Managed Services Buying Guide*:

> *Managing security risk can feel like climbing a mountain. The terrain is rocky and the grade is uneven. Conditions can change suddenly, making it difficult to reach your goal. Even the most*

experienced climbers travel together to share the burden.[40]

THE MUSE

Cheerful, pure and aspirational

The Muse inspires beauty, richness and imagination. In addition to tangible, measurable goals, The Muse emphasizes aspirational goals such as culture and happiness. The Muse makes customers feel inspired, hopeful and cool. Let's look at some examples of The Muse.

IKEA

IKEA's stated purpose isn't to sell furniture. It's to "create a better everyday life."[41] Sofas, bookcases and rugs are the tools IKEA uses to make this aspirational vision a reality. Not only does IKEA provide the DIY vision, it inspires customers to make their own creations with Ikea "hacks."

Slack

While the brand voice of Slack, a project management and collaboration tool for businesses, can be witty like The Jester, it's also super smart and inspiring. As The Muse, Slack has aspirational goals for changing the way people work. Slack is enjoyable to use, even addictive, which sets it apart from other enterprise software.

Slack's content choices reflect the emphasis on making the workday more productive and fun. The distinctive Slack voice is apparent on the company's website, blog, social media and, notably, within the product itself. The tagline "Be Less Busy," sets the tone and speaks to emotional needs in addition to career goals. Resources on the company's website include, "What digital transformation means for your company," and blogs that offer personal guidance, such as, "How feeling left out at work can affect your job."[42]

Slack is known as the fastest growing Software-as-a-Service (SaaS) company of all time. It's the most popular chat and productivity tool in the world, used by 77% of the Fortune 100.[43]

THE DEFENDER

Resolute and passionate, fighting for justice

The Defender is always on guard to protect customers against disaster or failure. He's dedicated to doing what it takes to make life easier and safer. The Defender makes customers feel comfortable, relieved, safe, protected and nurtured. Below are examples of Defender brands.

Method

Household cleaner company Method sells non-toxic laundry, dish and hand-and-body soaps. Method says its employees are "people against dirty" and invites customers to "leave the cleaning to us."[44]

In addition to defending against germs, the brand is also known as a defender of the environment, selling green cleaning products via an environmentally conscious supply chain.

With a differentiating mission and colorful, eco-friendly containers, Method built a strong fan base. Just five years after its launch, Method ranked seventh in the Inc. 500 ranking of fastest growing companies in the United States.[45] In 2012, when Method merged with Belgian company Ecover, it became the largest green cleaning company in the world[46], and in 2017, when purchased by SC Johnson, it became an important part of the household cleaning giant's move to offer more eco-friendly brands.[47]

Veracode

Cyber security company Veracode describes itself as "The Monster in your Corner," giving its customers powerful weapons to defend against cyber crime. On its website, Veracode shows photos of employees introduced as "Monsters."[48] Customers connect the brand's security expertise with real people working behind the scenes to keep them safe.

Veracode and its marketing partner PJA Advertising launched the "Monster" campaign with a website, print and banner ads, tradeshow designs, videos, and interactive content. As a result of the integrated campaign, 49.5% of target accounts increased engagement with Veracode, more than doubling the company's goal.[49]

STORY FROM THE TRENCHES

Jean Rosauer is the founder of marketing strategy firm Fuel Growth Group and formerly CMO of Tandberg and head of marketing for "Rebel" brand, Acano.

She shares her advices on selecting a brand archetype:

Stand out by being aspirational and bold in a crowded market. But don't fall down on credibility.

Not every company can or should be The Rebel, for example—at least not right away. Especially in the B2B world, many customers don't want to work with The Rebel because they're nervous about change and how change affects their own jobs. Unlike B2C buyers that may want to associate with something rebellious, many B2B buyers would rather play it safe.

Before you can position your company as The Rebel, make sure you gain your audience's trust. Be sure your products do what you say they do and have the customer stories to back up those claims.

But note that the rewards are great for a Rebel who also delivers amazing product or service performance. Your rebelliousness captures attention in a crowded market and your performance multiplies sales momentum. This can give anyone, but especially start-ups, an incredible boost in the market.

> *Video conferencing start-up Acano had the opportunity to enter an entrenched industry that hadn't changed in some time. We intentionally used language and showed examples that were very different from what people were used to seeing. The company was successful because customers were attracted to our fresh voice, and we gained momentum with a reliable, well-engineered product. Acano captured the market's attention and was sold to Cisco for $700 million.[50]*

Does more than one archetype seem like you?

Don't be afraid to incorporate aspects of more than one archetype to reflect your own brand personality, such as being The Guide with a "rebellious streak." Just as you act differently when you're with your grandmother than when you're with your friends, brands can emphasize or de-emphasize aspects of their personality depending on the audience and the situation. For example, you may discuss different elements of your solution or approach when talking with an executive versus one of the supporting staff.

In addition, you can communicate differently based on *where* you are, just as you may speak more casually when you're at home than when you're at work. As a brand, you may be more informal on social media but more formal when creating technical documentation.

That said, I wouldn't recommend mixing more than two archetypes or you will dilute your brand and confuse your audience. You shouldn't alter your core personality to the degree that people wouldn't recognize you.

What we covered:

- Brand archetypes tap into the subconscious of your customers.

- The six common archetypes have distinct perspectives, objectives and styles that set them apart.

- Understanding how archetypes are used in the real world helps your brand team hold a mirror up to your own organization and accelerate your brand development process.

What's next:

- An archetype gives you the bones of your brand personality, but it's just a skeleton. Next, we need to add some flesh and blood to make your brand personality more, well, *human*. We need to put some words in his mouth.

CHAPTER 5
WHAT YOU SAY

What you'll learn: *In this chapter you'll learn how to create a message architecture. You'll see how to build connections between your overarching brand personality and the more detailed marketing messages that support it.*

It's time to turn the skeleton of the brand archetype we discussed in the last chapter into a living, breathing, feeling, brand personality. To do this, we need to give him a "brand voice."

Your brand voice includes *what you say* as well as *how you say it*

What you say:

- Information you want to share with your target audience at different points in their journey with you.

- Topics you associate yourself with in your content marketing, blog and social media.

How you say it:

- Your word choice and sentence structure.

- Your writing style and tone.

- Format and delivery channels for your content.

This chapter gives you a template to architect **what you say**. In the next chapter we'll cover **how you say it.** Don't be tempted to rush ahead. There will be time for shaping and smoothing out language later on. Skipping the messaging step is like getting dressed with only accessories and forgetting the clothes. Please—don't go outside undressed.

What is a message architecture?

A message architecture is a hierarchical framework for your communication. Within this structure, messages you want to share with customers are listed in order of priority and supported by specific examples, sometimes called "proof points."

The process I recommend for building your messaging architecture is an example of working from the ground up. You start with the details, then prioritize and finally distill.

If you've been spending all your time at the high level, this can feel like a jump, especially if you're working with a large company with diverse markets, products and customers. You don't need to try and tackle all messages for the entire company at a time. Start with a single business unit. A single product. A single persona in your buying cycle. Particularly if you work within a product-based company, this is where those product managers and product marketing managers in your brand SWAT team are key participants to bridge the gap between high level branding and messaging and positioning related to different offerings.

First, list all potential messages your company wants customers to know about you, your products and services, and your position in the market relative to competitors. Of course there are many things you want to express to your customers. But not all messages are equal.

Prioritize three key messages. Keeping the number small and the messages concise will make it easier for everyone in your organization to remember and deliver them consistently.

To prioritize key messages from your list, flip the perspective. Ask:

- *What hot-button topics are customers most worried about that need to be addressed?*

- *Why are you the best choice for the future?*

- *How do you set yourself apart?*

If these questions sound familiar it's because this is where you bring together the three building blocks of your brand personality we covered in depth in Chapter 2: culture, customers and competition.

The message test

For a message to rise to the level of a "key message," it needs to pass the message test.

Is it true?

Whatever you say about your organization should be authentic. Think about whether a message is a match with your brand personality. Is it something that personality would consider highly important? For example, one of the key messages "The Defender" archetype likes to talk about is "safety," right? So, if that is you, make sure at least one of your key messages emphasizes how your organization keeps customers safe.

Can you prove it?

Some of your marketing messages may sound nice but don't have legs. That means no one will remember a message if you can't provide specifics. Even if *you* know something to be true, if you can't back up what you say, customers will be skeptical. Choose key messages you can support with examples, testimonials from clients or data points.

Is it unique?

If a message is something others in your industry could also say, customers consider it "table stakes." It's the minimum requirement to compete for their attention. Generic messages like these only dilute your brand. Your goal is to prioritize messages that are unique to you.

Is it something customers really care about?

Just because you think something is important enough for your brand personality to talk about doesn't mean your customers care about it. Go back to your customer research and interviews and ensure that each key message you've listed reflects their concerns.

Worksheet: Marketing Message Test

Plug each of your key messages into this checklist and confirm it passes the test. Then rank the messages to choose the top three.

	TRUE	PROVABLE	UNIQUE	CUSTOMER-CENTRIC
Message 1				
Message 2				
Message 3				
Message 4				
Message 5				
Message 6				

Multiple buyers in your sales process?

B2B marketers have unique challenges. They're often removed from customer interactions and have to dig deeper than B2C marketers to discover what customers want to hear. Many B2B sales processes involve multiple buyers who may need to hear different messages. Once a B2B sale is complete, the actual *users* of a product or service are often an entirely different set of people. These factors can make the job of creating a messaging architecture more challenging—but not impossible!

If you sell your offerings to different types of buyers, you'll want to craft messages that address each of their pain points and objectives. The format below forces you to think first about what each type of customer would ask if he was in the room with your brand. Your messages and supporting points follow, according to each customer's priorities.

Below is a sample messaging architecture used by a marketing services company with two different types of buyers, the brand marketer and the e-commerce manager. Each buyer has a different section of the architecture structured as an imaginary conversation he or she has with your brand personality.

Worksheet: Customer-centric Message Architecture

TARGET BUYER 1 **BRAND MARKETER**	BRAND X ADDRESSES THESE NEEDS BECAUSE WE...	AS PROOF OF OUR CAPABILITIES, BRAND X...
I care about ... increasing brand awareness with new audiences.	A—aren't limited to display ads like other vendors; we also offer social and search advertising. B—help you better understand your target customers' attributes, behaviors and preferences. C—have unique targeting capabilities to reach new prospects.	I—can demonstrate an increase in web traffic coming from first-time visitors. II—can demonstrate conversions that come from first-time visitors vs. returning visitors. III—is the only company with proprietary data that identifies customer behavior and buying patterns.

TARGET BUYER 2 **E-COMMERCE MANAGER**	BRAND X ADDRESSES THESE NEEDS BECAUSE WE...	AS PROOF OF OUR CAPABILITIES, BRAND X...
I care about ... lowering costs/managing my budget efficiently.	A—receive payment when our efforts result in a sale. B—place no limit on creative and technical tests, optimizations or campaign adjustments. C—have no requirements for length of our service agreement.	I—typically lowers cost per acquisition for customers by 40%.

You can add on sections for different buyer personas and add on rows for marketing messages as you need.

When you break each message down in this format you can immediately see where you have gaps in your information and where you need to add more specifics or more punch. When you have a robust row, chock full of examples and differentiating proof points, you know your message is a winner.

Finally, distill your key messages into a single value proposition

A value proposition, sometimes called your "elevator pitch," takes the most important messages and distills them into a single descriptive paragraph. In the simplest terms, your value proposition explains what you do, highlighting the *value* that you provide to customers.

It isn't a *tagline*, which is a catchy, short phrase like Nike's "Just Do It." Rather, a value proposition is typically a one-to three-sentence paragraph. It's short enough to force prioritization and focus. And it's long enough to be packed with meaning.

To be potent, a value proposition must offer specifics:

- *Who* benefits from your products or services.

- *How* you help customers overcome challenges and meet their goals.

- *Why* your product or approach is different and better than anyone else's.

A generic, bland value proposition just lies there on the page. As an example, let's dissect a value proposition that needs some love. Take 1:

We improve the quality of education.

This could be any type of education company, right? We don't know what type of people this company helps or what specific help people receive. The word "quality" sounds like something good for customers, but it doesn't tell them exactly what it means or how they should measure it.

How can you make this value proposition jump off the page? Add some specifics. Take 2:

We provide a comprehensive library of easy-to-manage, personalized video-based learning tools for K-12 schools.

Now the value proposition includes:

- **Who customers are:** K-12 schools.

- **What the company provides:** Video-based learning.

- **What the competitive differentiator is:** From this statement we can assume similar tools aren't as easy to use.

This value proposition is better than the first, but it's still too weak to influence anyone. It doesn't explain why customers should care about this approach or confirm why they should buy from this particular company. It doesn't ignite a spark. Take 3:

We empower K-12 teachers to help students become active learners. Our easy-to-use, video-based learning tools boost student engagement by five times. We're the only video solution that adapts to a student's specific learning challenges.

Now we know:

- **What benefits to expect:** Students become active learners.

- **How we can measure this:** Engagement increases five times!

- **Why this company:** This time we don't have to guess at the competitive differentiators. The company tells us why it's better than the competition. It's easy and, most importantly, it adapts to different students.

What we covered:

- How to structure a messaging architecture.

- How to prioritize messages based on the three building blocks.

- How to distill messages in a single, influential value proposition.

What's next:

Keep in mind, a message architecture is a framework that tells you **what to say** to different people in your target audience. But it's not marketing copy. It's the basis from which marketing copy is created.

We still have the other half of the equation to go: ***how you say it***. In the next chapter we'll talk about how to express marketing messages with the tone and style of your brand personality.

CHAPTER 6
HOW YOU SAY IT

What you'll learn: *In this chapter you'll learn how to create content worthy of your brand personality and powerful techniques that make your content more readable and engaging.*

It's time to flex some writing muscle. Your brand personality includes not only the key messages you emphasize, but also the language choices you make. This includes the words you use as well as their order, rhythm and pace.

Here is an everyday example of how a simple request can be articulated in different ways:

- "You wouldn't happen to have a spare pencil, would you?"

- "Do you have a pencil I can borrow?"

- "Gimme that pencil."

Same meaning. Different feeling. Even from a few words you immediately form an impression of the person who is talking.

How does your brand talk?

You have some decisions to make about your brand voice.

Word and sentence length

Brands that present themselves as simple and direct tend to use shorter words and sentences. For example, politicians tend to speak this way with the goal of presenting themselves as honest and accessible, even "folksy." On the other hand, brands that want to convey sophistication and nuance may use more complex words and sentences.

Pronouns

"Your choice of pronouns can have a big effect on your tone," explains Dr. Andrew Bredenkamp for the Content Marketing Institute. "For example, when writing about your company, you can use first person (*we*) or third person (*Acme Corporation*). First person is more immediate, positioning your brand as a group of people, while third person is more detached and abstract, with less clarity as to who is speaking. When referencing your audience, you can use second person (*you*) or third person (*customers* or *suppliers*). Second person is direct and engaging, while third person is more distanced."[51]

Contractions

A more relaxed, casual brand personality will typically use contractions to make readers feel they're engaging in a conversation.

Colloquialisms

Colloquial language is the language of a specific culture. It can include expressions, slang and even profanity. As in the example of Target and its awkward hashtags, you need to understand how your audience will receive the use of colloquial language before you start shooting from the hip.

Industry jargon

It's very tempting for B2B companies, especially technology firms, to use industry jargon in an effort to appear authoritative. If your audience understands the terms, it's fine to use some jargon when it adds needed context and detail. But, relying on industry jargon as a crutch can get in the way of connecting with your audience and makes it difficult to differentiate your company from other vendors in your industry.

Techniques to make your writing more powerful

For most companies, your customers will first experience your brand personality in a written format, likely through your website, advertisement, email or social media. If they meet you at an event, they'll first see your description in the program or pass by your booth display. Before they talk to the people behind the brand, they'll form a first impression.

Regardless of what type of brand personality you're working to convey, the words you write need to have "weight" in order to be memorable and influential. Marketing expert Ann Handley says they need to be "heavy enough to hurt when you drop them on your foot."[52] How can your writing put on the pounds?

Active voice vs. passive voice

A passive sentence ("It is recommended that our product be installed by a professional,") sounds like you are hiding something. Who is making this recommendation? If it's you, stand up and say so! ("We recommend a professional install the product.") Or, better yet, cut out the extra words and just say what you mean as directly as you can. ("Have a professional install the product.")

Action verbs

Whenever possible, try to banish words like "is," "has," "do," "may" or "will." Action verbs include more information about how an activity is conducted and clues about the person conducting it. For example, writing that someone "said" something is pretty generic. But if you say they "insisted," your reader instantly understands the importance of the statement and gets a sense of the person making it.

Words that call on the senses

Do you have a physical product? Describe how it feels to hold it, press the buttons, hear the sounds it makes. Do you write a blog? Describe an experience that relates to your topic and include the sights, sounds and smells.

Imagery and analogies

Reference well-known concepts and examples. If you say something is 100 yards long, it's hard for a reader to visualize. But if you say it's "as long as a football field," the reader gets an immediate mental image that supports the information.

Harness the power of storytelling

Countless marketers, advertisers, writers and psychologists have written about the power of storytelling to engage and motivate an audience. The best description I've seen of why this works comes from Forbes.

> *"First, there's cortisol, which gets produced when something warrants our attention, like distress. Where we hear about potential threats in our environment—or hear something distressing in a story—cortisol helps us stay attentive. From a marketer's perspective, cortisol may be the compound most closely associated with the 'top of the funnel' experience—the first contact with a customer—known as awareness.*

Next comes a far more popular compound—so much has been written about it—called dopamine. This gets produced to aid in an elaborate learning system that rewards us (with pleasure) when we follow the emotionally charged events in a story. This takes us further down the funnel. If cortisol helps with awareness, dopamine aids, so to speak, with arousal, rewarding us to stick with the journey.

And then comes what could very well be the wonder drug of storytelling: oxytocin. While there are many other things in the human organism that help make us social, oxytocin has been identified as a chemical that promotes prosocial, empathic behavior. And according to the story scientists, it's what enables us to identify with the hero/protagonist in a story."[53]

Any brand personality can use storytelling techniques as long as the stories you tell reflect the essence of your brand. Storytelling is particularly effective for an in-person format like a sales meeting or event presentation or longer content like e-books, videos or blogs. You can incorporate storytelling in your writing in a number of ways.

The only requirement for a story is that it ring true. It must be about people in real-life situations experiencing genuine emotions.

Humanize your brand with personal anecdotes

When you describe your own experience struggling with a challenge, you make yourself relatable to your audience. They think, "Hey, she's just like me." The key is to show how you overcame challenges to benefit yourself and your audience. This gets your reader thinking, "Wow, if she could do this, I could do this too."

Some brands call on their "origin story" to humanize their brand. This works particularly well for small businesses or organizations where the founder has an inspiring story. Even a short anecdote, like the one TOMS includes on its website, helps to humanize the brand.

> *While traveling in Argentina in 2006, TOMS Founder Blake Mycoskie witnessed the hardships faced by children growing up without shoes. Wanting to help, he created TOMS Shoes, a company that would match every pair of shoes purchased with a new pair of shoes for a child in need. One for One®.*

> *What began as a simple idea has evolved into a powerful business model that helps address need and advance health, education and economic opportunity for children and their communities around the world.*[54]

Invite your reader behind the scenes

Give your readers a glimpse of the inner workings of your organization. Find behind-the-scenes stories only your brand can tell. You don't have to reserve these stories for the About Us or Careers page. Apple used a storytelling technique in the launch of its new earbuds, describing exactly how the development process resulted in a more durable, stable product.

> *Apple engineers asked more than 600 people to test over 100 iterations of the Apple EarPods. Testers ran on treadmills in extreme heat and extreme cold. They performed various cardio workouts. They were even asked to shake their heads side to side, up and down. The result: Apple EarPods provide stronger protection from sweat and water, and they're remarkably stable in the ear. Which means they stay in, even when you're on the go.*[55]

Use nut grafs to illustrate a trend

"Nut graf" is an editorial term used by journalists. The term refers to a paragraph or sentence that delivers a promise of the story's content and message. It's called the nut graf because, like a nut, it contains the "kernel" of the story.

Network Alliance, a Centerboard Marketing client, uses this technique within its blog by including a quick personal story and then pivoting to a nut graf containing a larger issue that impacts all its target customers.

Tom Wilmer, CEO of Axeo, only carries his iPad to client meetings and accesses all of his presentations as if he were in the office. For Tom's HR consulting practice, full mobility is essential.

Axeo is part of a growing number of businesses that offer "Bring Your Own Device (BYOD)" flexibility, a trend that's changing the way people work in all types of companies.[56]

Worksheet: How Brands Talk

To demonstrate how a key message can be expressed in a variety of ways by different brand personalities, let's take a message that many companies want to convey:

"Our product is easy to use."

Below are the six common archetypes that form the basis for most brand personalities, and their defining characteristics. See how each archetype makes intentional language choices to infuse their personality into the message?

BRAND PERSONALITY	PERSONALITY TRAITS	HOW THEY MIGHT SAY IT
The Pioneer	First to do something, truth-telling, optimistic.	"We discovered a newer, easier way of doing things."
The Rebel	Aggressively undoing wrongs, potentially controversial or counter culture.	"Throw out the complex tools you hate to use."
The Guide	Experienced, confident leader, trusted advisor.	"Let us show you an easier way to achieve your goals."
The Jester	Whimsical, playful, quirky.	"So ridiculously easy even a three-year old can do it."
The Muse	Cheerful, pure, aspirational.	"So easy it's invisible."
The Defender	Resolute, passionate, fighting for justice.	"We make life easy for you."

Choose the right format for your personality

Reflect back on the brand touchpoint list from Chapter 2. As you review and revamp your brand touchpoints to match your brand personality, consider which formats fit best.

A brand based on The Guide may create thought leadership content like how-to advice and original research. Customer service software provider HelpScout has built a great example of an online resource center that's designed to be educational rather than promotional.[57]

A brand based on The Jester may come up with quirky quizzes or contests. For example, SnapApp helps many companies create playful, visually compelling interactive tools for websites and social media. A fun example is their own "Content Land: An Interactive Quest."[58]

If the service or product you offer is a new concept, your audience may need some help imagining themselves using it. A brand based on The Muse often creates conceptual videos that portray a vision of the future. Corning, a Centerboard Marketing client, created a visionary *Day Made of Glass* video series which draws viewers into a future where every aspect of their lives incorporates glass as a surface for communication—from planning their schedule on their bathroom mirror to shopping in an interactive dressing room, to watching TV on the window while a passenger in a car.[59]

A brand based on The Rebel gravitates toward experiential marketing that reflects its nature to break out of the typical marketing techniques. Take, for example, the *Fearless Girl* statue. State Street Global Advisors, a financial services company, installed the bronze statue of a ponytailed girl staring down a bull near Wall Street as part of an initiative to encourage companies to put women on their boards. It became an iconic symbol of the gender-equality movement.

What we covered:

- Make your writing more powerful with unique, evocative language.

- Integrate storytelling techniques to humanize your brand and engage readers.

- Reflect your brand personality in the content format you choose.

What's next:

- It's time to put everything together and share it with the world!

CHAPTER 7
ALL SYSTEMS GO

What you'll learn*: In this chapter we'll cover how to roll out your brand personality to the world. You'll hear about companies that have executed brand launches and learn what worked and what pitfalls to avoid.*

Congratulations on your journey of self-discovery! Now that you've got a clear vision of your brand personality, it's time to put it into action.

I like to use a multi-phase rollout to make sure an organization is primed before releasing a new brand personality to the rest of the world. By separating internal and external launches, an organization is better prepared to communicate the brand personality and feels included in something special.

During the brand development process, your core team has been through a lot together. You know the history of the discussions you've had and the hard choices you've made. You've developed a shorthand and can jump into the middle of a discussion about the brand without any preamble. You've come to think of your brand personality as a friend.

Others haven't been behind the scenes for every decision. When it comes time to roll out the brand personality to your wider organization, remember that other people don't know everything you know.

Think back to the parable in Chapter 2 about "burning the boats" to force a brand refresh. As Cameron Caswell of Synopsys advises, "you can't take away people's boats without giving them new boats to use." In other words, if you expect the rest of your organization to execute on the new brand personality, you need to empower them to do so. "Make sure people have the tools they need and remove all friction to using the new brand," she warns, "or they aren't going to do it."[60]

To help your organization transition, you need to put a few crucial things in place.

First, arm the content creators

As you're preparing your brand launch, you'll be writing and designing numerous marketing and sales materials. When multiple people become involved in the process, including in-house and external copywriters and graphic designers, inconsistencies can creep in. Especially during the first few months of crafting content to reflect the defined brand personality, an extended team will need extra support to stay on target.

I help content creators get started on the right track with a few key tools.

Brand book

A brand book acts as a single source of truth on your brand personality. It doesn't need to be a tome. You simply need a single location where all your brand materials live so that anyone in your company and your partners and contactors can reference them.

It should include the description of your brand personality along with the key character traits and emotions you strive to evoke in your audience. Your message architecture should be included—at least at a high level. Focus on the foundational elements such as your value proposition and key messages. Any visual brand identity elements you've developed, such as colors, logo, typeface and photography style, should be included as well.

Writer's style guide

The style guide can be a part of the brand book, but I like to break this out as a specific asset in order to make sure it gets into the hands of writers and goes into the depth that writers need. Don't leave your writers hanging with a vague instruction to be more "transparent and approachable." A writer's guide must explore the nuances and connotations of language choices and include specific examples and comparisons.

Content training

Hold training sessions for content creators. I like to record these so an organization can share the session with new employees, subject matter experts who may only occasionally contribute content, or external contractors.

Remember, not all content is managed via the marketing team. Product folks also create technical documents and in-product language like error messages. Include those types of content creators in your trainings as well.

In the training session, go through examples of content that reflect the brand personality as well as content that doesn't. Show how content could be revised to hit the mark.

Review process

If you don't already have a review process for content, a brand update gives you an opportunity to institute new ways of doing things. Before any new content is added to the editorial calendar, and again before it's published, someone who knows the brand personality inside and out should review and sign off.

Next, hold department-specific rollout sessions

It's a good idea to hold dedicated sessions with particular groups in your organization that carry heavy responsibility for expressing the brand personality in their day-to-day work.

If you've followed the activities outlined in this book, many employees outside the core SWAT team have been involved in different aspects of the brand process and these rollout sessions won't hit them by surprise.

Salespeople

Salespeople are a key group responsible for delivering the brand story directly to customers.

One of the most effective sales presentation training approaches I've seen comes from my time working with education company Blackboard. When we launched a new sales presentation format and story, we held a video contest for the sales team. Everyone was asked to record themselves delivering the new pitch. Salespeople were required to follow the basic format and key messages, but could adjust the core story using their own presentation style and examples from their own experience. The sales leadership team judged the videos and awarded a prize to the most effective presentation.

Customer support

Technical and customer service departments often speak or chat online with customers when those customers are stressed. How employees handle those conversations reflects your company's brand personality.

If you've called into the Zappos customer service line, you get what I mean. Zappos embraces service as a core tenant of its brand personality. It captures and shares stories of its employees going the extra mile to humanize its brand.[61]

Zappos is so committed to delivering great customer service that it built a training program, the School of WOW, to help other companies "build personal emotional connections and provide WOW service through empowerment and ownership."[62]

Human Resources

The Human Resources department is responsible for introducing the brand personality to prospective employees and new hires. Show them how the corporate brand personality relates to a "talent brand" that helps them attract and retain the strongest talent.

Foundation Medicine is an example of a company with a brand-aligned recruiting strategy. The company is dedicated to providing personalized and unique treatment to cancer patients. It launched an employer branding campaign to attract job candidates with a video incorporating personal stories from employees and a #uniquelyFMI hashtag. The personal nature of messages in the videos and social media match the brand personality and key message of the company.[63]

Third, ensure everyone throughout your organization feels included

Including all employees in the launch of your brand personality can go a long way toward making them feel they've got a stake in the brand's success. You may have to get creative to reach all employees, especially if you have a dispersed organization, but it's worth the effort. Below are some internal launch tactics to inspire you:

Hold all-hands sessions in person or online

Use the opportunity to gather everyone together to emphasize the importance of the brand personality to your organization. This is a great chance for the executive sponsor to describe a bit of the process and the plans for the rollout.

Shape your environment

Put up posters around the office. Stick some "flush facts" about your brand personality on the inside of bathroom stalls. Let's say your brand personality is based on The Rebel archetype. Maybe you cover your office walls in quotes from famous rebels, describing the value of breaking the mold. The Pioneer might rename meeting rooms as "Lewis and Clark" or "Ponce de Leon."

Create a video

An internal video that includes people from all areas of your organization can be a fun and authentic way to describe the brand personality.

Hand out free stuff

Who doesn't love free stuff? To mark the occasion, you can give every employee something that reinforces the brand personality. On the morning of the company's brand relaunch, SurveyMonkey employees got swag:

> "Cool T-shirts, a notebook and pen, a handy pocket brand book, and a Rubik's cube-like code game designed to spark their curiosity. SurveyMonkey's mission is to 'Power the Curious,' and even little things like puzzle games (for prizes, of course) can help drive that point home."[64]

Finally, you're ready to launch *externally*

With your internal organization primed, you can now tell the rest of the world. Depending on the scope of your update and whether you've chosen a brand relaunch or refresh, you may decide to phase your external rollout, first to a trusted group and then to everyone else.

Give your inner circle a sneak peek

If you have a group of trusted external advisors, such as a customer council or channel partners, you can provide them a sneak peek. This tactic works particularly well if you're revealing a new brand before an industry event or otherwise making a big, public splash.

Arm your brand ambassadors

Pick a group of influencers within your community, those who are active on social media. If you're hosting an industry or customer event, give them a front-row seat. Dub them "guest bloggers" and have them comment and share their insights on your brand. Go out of your way to thank them and make sure they feel special and appreciated.

Go live!

If you've chosen a full brand update, your goal is to have all brand elements go live at once. If you're managing a phased brand refresh, your goal is a smooth transition over time. Either way, the first day you launch a new brand personality is an exciting time. By the time you get here, you should feel confident that your new brand personality is strong and sustainable, ready to carry your organization into the future.

STORY FROM THE TRENCHES

Jackie Yeaney is the Chief Marketing Officer (CMO) of Ellucian, where she is responsible for all aspects of marketing, including marketing strategy and communications, brand, solutions marketing, marketing operations and field marketing. A former marketing leader at Red Hat and Delta Air Lines, she recently led Ellucian through a brand revitalization journey.

Higher education technology giant Ellucian formed in 2011 from the merger of two industry leaders, SunGard and Datatel. It launched with an intriguing name and bold purple color, but lacked a framework to communicate what those brand elements represented. When CMO Jackie Yeaney joined Ellucian in 2017, she and her team needed to fill in the gaps with a brand platform that unites its 3,000+ employees and inspires tens of thousands of customers and end users.

"In order to get our marketing strategy right, I needed to focus on this first. A brand platform is the foundation upon which we build everything else," Jackie explains. She made the bold decision to put a website refresh project on hold until she knew it could be built based on a meaningful, consistent brand.

A brand awakening

Rather than a brand "definition," Jackie calls the process "a brand awakening—an exercise in self-discovery that uncovered our true identity and what the world would lose if Ellucian didn't exist."

Over several months, the team spoke with internal employees and customers to understand the goals and emotions that drive their decisions.

One word kept coming up: passion.

"At first, I didn't believe that a company could be defined by a passion for a category," Jackie admits. "But Ellucian—where people have worked in education for 15 to 20 years—is different from broad technology companies and tiny tech companies. We hit above our weight in terms of talent. Being mission-oriented really resonates with customers and helps them understand who we are. This wasn't a huge shift in our personality. It gave people permission to be who they are and to act on it."

The team tested marketing messages and wording to prioritize the most authentic, most meaningful choices. As Jackie describes, "Listening to customers was incredibly important. It was an 'aha' moment for me when customers said they didn't want us to say our mission is student success. Ultimately, it is their job to educate. It is our job to empower and enable them. That customer feedback changed the words we use and put the institution at the center."

A detailed and nuanced brand framework boils down to the Ellucian brand essence: powered by our passion for higher education.

Internal rollout

"We spent four to five months before our external rollout obsessed with the internal work," Jackie says. "Our brand comes from a shared belief system. Our goal is to have people feel it, not just say it. That's why it's important to 'Be' and 'Do' the brand before you 'Say' it.

For a brand to be successful, people need to be able to articulate it in a sentence or two. Once people understand what that means, they can make decisions in their own work. We don't expect everyone to use exactly the same words or do exactly the same things. It's the idea of the brand that's important."

During the internal rollout Ellucian held workshops with executives and key departments to help them understand and incorporate the brand in their everyday behaviors. The marketing team held writing classes. The customer renewal team revamped the tone of voice of renewal notices. The event team focused on setting up an environment that facilitated more conversations with booth visitors instead of simply clicking badges.

As organizations get larger, Jackie notes, brand "awakenings" are more about change management than they are about marketing.

"It's important for people to feel part of the process," Jackie advises. "In the past we created a 'mirror room' where we posted all of the things our customers had to say about us and invited people to come in and see for themselves. It's especially important to bring along the key influencers across the company in your process. If you get them on board, others will also be far more likely to join. You can't afford to have internal influencers as blockers."

External rollout

The revitalized Ellucian brand came to life at Ellucian Live, an annual user conference with 8,000+ customers. The design became more sophisticated with angular lines, a deeper purple and more extensive color palette. While the logo didn't change, Ellucian added a "bug" ahead of its name—a symbol tilted at 68 degrees, reflecting the year of the original company's founding. It is meant to represent a power button and the letter 'e.'

Of course the brand rollout was much more than a design change. Several sessions at the conference transitioned from technology-oriented topics to broader discussions of student experience and campus leadership, demonstrating Ellucian's commitment and passion.

At the end of 2018, Ellucian launched its new website. The site is designed to convey the brand personality and make an emotional connection, with compelling video content, interactive tools, and success stories reflecting different types of institutions. "In our increasingly complicated world people make their vendor decisions more based on brand, emotion and trust, not simply features and functions. You choose a product or solution when the features are close enough to what you need, but then that final decision is based more on emotional factors," Jackie notes.

The rollout continues as Ellucian listens and learns from employees and customers. Instead of an all-at-once refresh, the team creates new content and updates materials continually. Jackie's advice is, "don't obsess about getting voice and tone perfect or you'll get stuck. Start and then keep evolving."

Measuring success

Ellucian measures the success of its brand work both quantitatively and qualitatively. "We ask people how well they understand the brand in our employee engagement surveys, and we see how scores go up. We get external validation from market brand tracker studies we do every 12-18 months," Jackie notes.

More importantly, employees contend that marketing isn't anything like it used to be. "Employees have latched onto the brand," she says. "There is genuine excitement."[65]

DON'T FORGET TO CELEBRATE!

You and the brand team have worked hard to get to this day. Take a breath and mark your accomplishment. Make sure to thank everyone involved. You've flexed your creative muscle, overcome challenges and stretched yourselves in new ways.

Congratulations!

What we covered:

- Break your rollout into internal and external phases.

- Set up processes to keep your brand expression authentic and consistent.

What's next:

In our final chapter we'll talk about how to continually refine your brand personality as your organization and your customers evolve.

CHAPTER 8
CONCLUSION

You wake up the morning after your brand launch party, the sun is shining, the birds are singing and you think, "Wow, I have nothing left to do." Said no one, ever.

All brands need ongoing development and caretaking.

So, what should you do next?

Keep up the content engine

Now that you've built interest in your brand, keep up the momentum with a steady stream of fresh content. Use content to reach new audiences, reinforce your key messages and reposition yourself against competitors.

Track and share your success

Go back to your original communication goals from Chapter 1 and gather data to track changes. Depending on your business, you may be able to notice changes within a few weeks or a few months.

After you launched your brand personality, did your lead quantity or quality improve? Did your customer retention rates increase? Did you save time creating content? If you've been conducting win/loss interviews or measuring social media sentiment over time, compare results before and after the brand changes. Don't be shy about sharing results.

Employ brand as a decision-making tool

When a brand is embraced by an entire organization it can be used as a business decision-making tool. When evaluating whether your company should develop a new product, enter a new market or form a new partnership, your team can and should consider if it's a good fit for your company's brand.

Explore new brand extensions. At launch, you may have addressed only your most essential brand touchpoints or covered all of them. But you can count on the fact that new ones will surface. You'll look back at the core elements of your brand personality to make ongoing decisions about things like product naming, co-branding and marketing channels.

For example, only a few years ago, only the most cutting-edge companies were using chatbots or conversational interfaces. Now, more companies are writing skills for Alexa and integrating digital assistants that talk—not just figuratively, but literally! You'll need to decide if and how these new methods of communication fit with your brand personality.

Embrace change

Your brand isn't static. Brand development is a constant process of learning and refining. From this point forward, you'll be reshaping, rethinking and distilling.

Even if you followed the process in this book to a T and you've done rounds of testing with your target audience, once your brand is out in the wild, you'll hear feedback you didn't anticipate. Some messages will work and some will fall flat, but you'll be constantly learning and improving. Take it all in.

Over time, new people coming into your organization may shift the company culture. Competitors may emerge and change the market dynamics. Customers will change their expectations. Be open to letting things evolve.

Depending on the pace of change, you may revisit the brand personality process often, starting once more with the building blocks. Each time you go through it, the muscles will get stronger and stronger.

Bring your brand band back together on a regular basis to wrestle with questions that arise. Refine materials as you need. Your brand book and writer's guide should be living documents that adapt as you learn and grow.

Through this process, you'll notice emotional changes in your own organization as well. You'll discover hidden strengths and align your organization so you're stronger and faster than before. You may not have to repeat the full process from end to end and you may move more quickly to decision points.

In my experience, what separates lackluster brands from extraordinary ones is the willingness to listen. Listen to customers and empathize with their pain. Listen to competitors and reflect honestly on your own positioning. Listen to your organization and embrace your culture, history and values.

If you can do those things, the brand personality you present to the world will align your organization, bring customers to you and leave competitors in the dust.

Your brand personality is unique to you. It reflects your vision, culture, stories and connections you make with people.

Own it.

ACKNOWLEDGMENTS

Thank you to my family, Arthur, Abigail and Nathaniel Agin, for the endless support.

And thanks to my editors, first readers, fellow marketers and contributors whose wise feedback helped to shape the book: Josh Poltilove, Ellen Poltilove, Arthur Agin, Payal Diaz, Devra First, Maggie Whittier, Jean Rosauer, Matt Scherrer, Rebecca Chanin, Genevieve Concannon, Stacy Del Gallo, Jackie Yeaney, Ali Robinson, Cameron Caswell, Lise Cartwright and Allison Bosworth.

ABOUT THE AUTHOR

Award-winning marketer Margie Agin helps companies clarify their brand positioning, develop content-driven campaigns and accelerate sales. She is the founder of Centerboard Marketing, a marketing consultancy located in the Washington, D.C. area since 2012. She previously led marketing teams at Blackboard and Cisco and taught content marketing at Johns Hopkins University.

Throughout a career spanning more than 20 years, Margie has combined curiosity about people, strategic thinking, research, and sharp writing to help companies build exceptional marketing programs. When she's isn't busy wrangling a business and two kids, she also speaks at conferences, teaches, cooks, and travels whenever possible. Margie is a proud graduate of Tufts University and American University. She lives in Falls Church, Va., with her husband Arthur, daughter Abigail and son Nathaniel.

To learn more about Margie and Centerboard Marketing visit www.centerboard-marketing.com.

GET YOUR FREE ACTION GUIDE

As a way of saying thanks for your purchase, this book includes a free action guide that's exclusive to readers of *Brand Breakthrough*.

It's in a workbook format so you can apply the information you've learned in this book and kickstart your brand journey.

Get immediate access to the guide here:

www.centerboard-marketing.com/brand-breakthrough-action-guide/

THANK YOU

Thanks for reading!

If you enjoyed the book, please leave a review for *Brand Breakthrough* on Amazon.

I'd love to hear how your company's brand personality takes shape. Please drop me a note any time with your questions or wins at:

margie@centerboard-marketing.com

NOTES

1. Welch, Patrick, "Moneyball: Use Content Intelligence and Analytics to Build a Successful Sales Team," *Content Marketing Institute*, February 6, 2015, contentmarketinginstitute.com/2015/02/moneyball-content-sales-team/.

2. Gordan, Eric, "Consumers Increasingly Distrust Brands And Advertising. Here Is Why," *Yocale*, July 29, 2017, business.yocale.com/consumers-increasingly-distrust-brands-and-advertising-here-is-why/.

3. *Global Brand Health Report*, Hired, 2018, hired.com/brand-health-report.

4. *Employer Brand Playbook*, LinkedIn, snap.licdn.com/microsites/content/dam/business/talent-solutions/global/en_US/c/pdfs/employer-brand-playbook-us-en.pdf.

5. *The Rebranding Guide*, Ignyte, 2016, vault.ignytebrands.com/dl/mEIoFOtzOj.

6. "Here's how the 'unlimited' plans from Verizon, AT&T, Sprint, and T-Mobile compare," *Business Insider*, December 24, 2018, www.businessinsider.com/unlimited-

plans-comparison-verizon-att-sprint-tmobile-2018-2#the-other-caveat-not-all-networks-are-created-equal-2.

7. "Getting the Most from Your Business WiFi," *Verizon*, business.verizon.com/smallbizresources/get-the-most-from-your-business-wifi. Accessed December 2018.

8. "Small Business," *Sprint*, smallbusiness.sprint.com/ideas/small-business-manifesto/#/. Accessed December 2018.

9. "Sprint Business Brand Launch," *Velocity Partners*, velocitypartners.com/work/sprint-business-launch/. Accessed January 2019.

10. Del Gallo, Stacy, April 9, 2014, Johns Hopkins University, Guest lecture.

11. Marshall, John F., "How Starbucks, Walmart And IBM Launch Brands Internally. And What You Can Learn From Them," *Forbes*, April 9, 2013, www.forbes.com/sites/onmarketing/2013/04/09/how-starbucks-walmart-and-ibm-launch-brands-internally-and-what-you-can-learn-from-them/#236efec45774.

12. Marshall, John F., "How Starbucks, Walmart And IBM Launch Brands Internally. And What You Can Learn From Them," *Forbes*, April 9, 2013, www.forbes.com/sites/onmarketing/2013/04/09/how-starbucks-walmart-and-ibm-launch-brands-internally-and-what-you-can-learn-from-them/#236efec45774.

13. "The Pointless Arrow Still Lives at Amtrak," *Amtrak in the Heartland*, csanders429.wordpress.com/2016/12/31/the-pointless-arrow-still-lives-at-amtrak/. Accessed January 2019.

14. "Slack's Editorial Soul: Anna Pickard on Writing the Brand Experience," *Contagious*, May 12, 2015, www.contagious.com/news-and-views/slacks-editorial-soul-anna-pickard-on-writing-the-brand-experience.

15. Handley, Ann, "Ann Handley on Why Jargon Can Be Detrimental to Your Brand Voice and Tone," *Marketo*, September 2018, blog.marketo.com/2018/09/ann-handley-on-why-jargon-can-be-detrimental-to-your-brand-voice-tone.html.

16. "Mailchimp Has a New Look," *Mailchimp*, mailchimp.com/resources/new-brand-announcement-2018/. Accessed November 2018.

17. Lischer, Brian, "10 Benefits of Building a Truly Authentic Brand," *Ignyte*, www.ignytebrands.com/10-benefits-of-building-a-truly-authentic-brand/. Accessed November 2018.

18. Caswell, Cameron, Personal interview, January 24, 2019.

19. McLeod, Saul, "Maslow's Hierarchy of Needs," *Simple Psychology*, 2018, www.simplypsychology.org/maslow.html.

20. Whittier, Maggie, Personal interview, November 7, 2018.

21. Worth, Lori, "Branding from the Inside Out," *Thinking Bigger*, Vol. 23, Issue 10, https://ithinkbigger.com/branding-inside/.

22. Nolan, Hamilton, "Target's Dumb Internal Guide to Millennials (and Other Generations)," *Gawker*, January 9, 2015, gawker.com/targets-dumb-internal-guide-to-millennials-and-other-g-1678496059.

23. Pathak, Shareen, "Bae, Is Your Social Media Strategy on Fleek?" *Digiday*, January 13, 2015, digiday.com/marketing/bae-social-media-strategy-fleek/.

24. Litsa, Tereza, "How Emotional Connection Increases Customer Satisfaction," *ClickZ*, September 15, 2016, www.clickz.com/how-emotional-connection-increases-customer-satisfaction/105775/.

25. Lucchese, Lauren, Interview by Vinish Garg, "Content Strategy in Financial Corporations," *Medium*, May 30, 2018, medium.com/content-conversations/content-strategy-in-financial-corporations-an-interview-with-lauren-lucchese-of-capital-one-c1acfa346220.

26. Mcleod, Saul, "Carl Jung," *Simply Psychology*, 2014, www.simplypsychology.org/carl-jung.html.

27. Ventura, Michael, "Every Business Has an Origin Story: A Lesson in Branding," *HubSpot*, May 29, 2018, blog.hubspot.com/marketing/origin-story-branding.

28. "Red Bull Creates Better Content Than You Do, Here's How They Do It," *MackCollier.co*, February 1, 2018, www.mackcollier.com/red-bull-content-marketing/.

29. Macleod, Duncan, "Virgin Flying in the Face of Ordinary," *Inspiration Room*, January 4, 2013, theinspirationroom.com/daily/2013/virgin-flying-in-the-face-of-ordinary/.

30. *Virgin Atlantic*, www.virginatlantic.com/us/en Accessed December 2018.

31. "Virgin Atlantic, Sustaining the Brand Promise: Case Study," *Marketing Society*, June 9, 2012, www.marketingsociety.com/the-library/2010-virgin-

atlantic-sustaining-brand-promise-case-study#gKqo6mBuIc5JPsyI.99.

32. Del Ray, Jason, "Warby Parker is valued at $1.75 billion after a pre-IPO investment of $75 million," *Recode*, March 14, 2018, www.recode.net/2018/3/14/17115230/warby-parker-75-million-funding-t-rowe-price-ipo.

33. "History," *Warby Parker*, www.warbyparker.com/history. Accessed December 2018.

34. Feldstein, Michael, "Canvas Surpasses Blackboard Learn in US Market Share," *e-Literate*, July 8, 2018, mfeldstein.com/canvas-surpasses-blackboard-learn-in-us-market-share/.

35. "About Us," *Canvaslms*, Instructure, www.canvaslms.com/about-us/. Accessed December 2018.

36. "QUIZ: Which Moo-phoria Flavor Should You Try Next?" *Ben & Jerry's*, www.benjerry.com/whats-new/2018/11/which-moo-phoria-flavor. Accessed December 2018.

37. Bloomstein, Margot, *Content Strategy at Work*, Elsevier, 2012.

38. *Weight Watchers*, www.weightwatchers.com. Accessed November 2015.

39. "About," *Invisionapp*, Invision, https://www.invisionapp.com/. Accessed December 2018.

40. *Managed Services Buying Guide*, Synopsys, 2016.

41. "This is Ikea," *Ikea*, www.ikea.com/ms/en_US/this-is-ikea/company-information/index.html. Accessed December 2018.

42. "What digital transformation means for your company," and "How feeling left out at work can affect your job," slackhq.com/, *Slack*. Accessed January 2019.

43. Shah, Hiten, "How Slack Became a $5 Billion Business by Making Work Less Boring," *The Startup*, August 7, 2018, medium.com/swlh/how-slack-became-a-5-billion-business-by-making-work-less-boring-f78bdad685c8.

44. Method, methodhome.com/. Accessed December 2018.

45. "Method Products, Inc. Ranks No. 7 on the 2006 Inc. 500 with Three-Year Sales Growth of 3,390.5%," *Business Wire*, August 23, 2006, www.businesswire.com/news/home/20060823005699/en/Method-Products-Ranks-No.-7-2006-500#.VYengev9dig.

46. Wong, Kristine, "Green cleaning company Method acquired by Ecover," *Greenbiz.com*, September 4, 2012, www.greenbiz.com/news/2012/09/04/method-acquired-by-ecover.

47. Dye, Jessica, "SC Johnson scoops up Method, Ecover cleaning-product brands," *Financial Times*, September 14, 2017, www.ft.com/content/258928f1-cf88-348c-9cc3-cc90ca4aca09.

48. "Meet the monsters," *Veracode*, www.veracode.com/about/meet-the-monsters. Accessed October 2018.

49. "Put a monster in your corner," *PJA Advertising*, www.agencypja.com/work/veracode/. Accessed January 2019.

50. Rosauer, Jean, Personal interview, November 30, 2018.

51. Bredenkamp, Andrew, "Don't Sound Like Everyone Else: 12 Essential Elements to Create a Consistent Brand Voice," *Content Marketing Institute*, March 26, 2015, contentmarketinginstitute.com/2015/03/consistent-brand-voice/.

52. Handley, Ann, Content Marketing Conference, May 4, 2018, Boston, Massachusetts, Keynote address.

53. Rodriguez, Giovanni, "This Is Your Brain On Storytelling: The Chemistry Of Modern Communication," *Forbes*, July 21, 2017, www.forbes.com/sites/giovannirodriguez/2017/07/21/this-is-your-brain-on-storytelling-the-chemistry-of-modern-communication/#ec84c9dc8650.

54. "About Toms," *Toms*, www.toms.com/about-toms. Accessed December 2018.

55. Kahn, Jordan, "Jony Ive explains design process of Apple's new EarPods," *9to5mac*, September 12, 2012, 9to5mac.com/2012/09/12/jony-ive-explains-design-process-of-apples-new-earpods-video/.

56. "Why BYOD Matters for Your Business," *Network Alliance*. Accessed December 2017.

57. "Resources," *HelpScout*, www.helpscout.net/resources/. Accessed December 2018.

58. "Content Land," *SnapApp*, info.snapapp.com/SA-Content-Land-LP.html. Accessed December 2018.

59. "A Day Made of Glass," *YouTube*, Uploaded by Corning, February 7, 2011, https://www.youtube.com/watch?v=6Cf7IL_eZ38.

60. Caswell, Cameron, Personal interview, January 24, 2019.

61 "10 Inspiring Zappos Customer Support Stories," *Infiit-O*, 2013, www.slideshare.net/InfinitOInc/10-inspiring-zappos-customer-support-stories.

62. "School of Wow," *Zappos*, www.zapposinsights.com/training/schoolofwow. Accessed December 2018.

63. "FM I AM," *YouTube*, Uploaded by Foundation Medicine, December 11, 2015, https://youtu.be/hC6HMMS_RVA.

64. Sun, Lee, "5 Tips for Rallying Employees Behind a Rebrand," Inside Design, *Invision*, April 23, 2018, invisionapp.com/inside-design/surveymonkey-rebrand/.

65. Yeaney, Jackie, Personal interview, December 5, 2018.

www.ingramcontent.com/pod-product-compliance
Lightning Source LLC
Chambersburg PA
CBHW071206050326
40689CB00011B/2254